Mini Pigs / Teacup Pigs All You Need To Know

The Essential Guide –
Food, Training, Health,
Everyday Care, Accessories
What to Expect

Mini Pigs, Teacup Pigs, Micro Pigs,
Miniature Pigs, Pocket Pigs

By Harriet Fields

Foreword

Teacup, Micro, Micro Mini, Pocket Pig, Dandie, Pixie, Designer Pig – meet the Micro Pigs. Adorable, intelligent, affectionate, the micro pig is an undeniably extremely rewarding pet. But, more than many other pets, the decision to commit to becoming a Piggy Parent is a huge one.

Indeed, adding a pig to your family is a life changing commitment. As a herd animal, your mini pig will consider you and your family as their herd. Finding its place in the herd will be complicated, for you and your pig.

Foreword

They will require plenty of interaction and stimulation to feel safe and secure. This is a journey of 15 years so be sure you are ready for the adventure.

This doesn't mean you should abandon your plans, just take your time to research the world of Micro Pigs and find out everything you can.

After all, if you love Micro Pigs and are passionate about them, you want to be sure that you are prepared for your new pet and are the best owner that you can be.

Indeed, if you are already the proud owner of a Micro Pig, the more informed you are, the better you will be as a Piggy Parent.

This book is designed to be easy to read and understand. As well as guiding you through the pros and cons of keeping a Micro Pig as a pet, this book will serve you throughout your time as a Micro Pig owner as a valuable and essential point of reference.

Contents

Contents

Contents

Contents

Contents

Chapter 1 – Meet the Micro Pigs

Wondering what the difference is between Micro, Mini, Miniature, Teacup Pig, Pocket Pig, Apartment Pig, Designer Pig, Dandy Pig, Royal Dandy? There is in fact no difference between these.

They are not specific breeds of pig, but are really adjectives used to describe or classify them in comparison to the larger breeds of pig. All of these terms have become an acceptable and widely used way to differentiate between pigs kept on farms and the smaller pigs kept as pets.

Chapter 1 – Meet the Micro Pigs

The Micro pigs include breeds of pigs that are smaller than the large pigs used in farming. The smaller breeds include Vietnamese Pot-bellied pigs, Kunekune, Juliana, American Guinea Hog, Ossabaw Island Hog (and also specimens resulting from cross breeding between these breeds).

Miniature Pigs can make a suitable pet if you are prepared, well informed and truly dedicated to being a responsible owner. Pigs are very intelligent animals which greatly explains why they can be such rewarding pets.

Like other pets, owning a micro pig is a responsibility and they do require daily attention and care. In the wild pigs would live in a herd – you and your family will be their herd and they will enjoy lots and lots of socialization with you.

Common Perceptions and Misperceptions

There are many myths about Micro Pigs and so let's explore some of these to find out which ones have some truth to them and which ones are false.

1 – Micro Pigs are Tiny

This is a misperception, perhaps the most common one and the one you really do need to be aware of. Micro pigs are smaller than pigs usually kept on farms, but this does not mean that they are tiny.

At birth, micro pigs really are tiny. Some pigs will remain small, but the overwhelming majority will grow much bigger than advertised or promised – or even guaranteed.

Pigs are not fully grown until the age of 3 – 5 years old. Interestingly they grow the most in their first 3 years. In technical terms, a pig has reached maturity when the epiphyseal plate in the long bones close meaning that they can grow no more. In general, this occurs when the pig is around 5 years old.

When a Mini Pig reaches maturity, it does not mean that your pig cannot grow heavier. This will continue whenever they intake more calories than they are using - just like ourselves! You can expect your Micro Pig to weigh between 75-200lbs.

The overall height and length of your Micro Pig will be very difficult to predict and will definitely be only an estimation. Later, we will talk about the specific breeds of pigs, so you can know more about what to expect.

2 – Pigs are Smelly and Unclean

This one is most certainly a myth. Pigs are in fact very clean animals. They will always do their toileting in a separate place to where they sleep and eat. Unlike many other animals (including pets that are very popular), pigs do not have their own scent.

This means that welcoming your micro pig to your home will not create an odor.

However, pigs do LOVE MUD! To enable your Micro Pig to keep cool in the warm summer months, your pig will need to be able to (and will LOVE to) wallow around in mud.

3 – Pigs are Slow Movers

This is another misperception! Consider the fact that in the wild pigs are prey animals. This means that they need to be able to run fast – it seems that running comes instinctively to them.

Some pigs have been known to run as fast as 11mph! It is thought that pigs in the wild can run even faster, as fast as 30 -35mph.

4 – Pet Pigs are very similar to pet dogs

The complexities of owning a pet pig should not be underestimated. The needs of a Micro Pig are far higher and very different to that of a dog.

Pigs are extremely intelligent animals and need a great deal of stimulation. As a Piggy Parent, you will need to provide stimulation and activities that will entertain your pig.

Although this will be very time consuming, you will be rewarded. It is important to note that if a pig becomes bored, it is likely that they will display destructive behavior.

5 – Pigs are aggressive

Providing you effectively meet the needs of your Micro Pig, this is not true. Further in this book we have a very in-depth and interesting look at the behavior of pigs ('Chapter 12 – Understanding Mini Pig Behavior and Training).

It is worth noting your Micro Pig may show aggressive tendencies as they become sexually mature. This can also be said of a dog. However, to avoid this (as with dogs), you will be able to spay or neuter your Micro Pig.

Another reason a pig may display aggressive behavior is if the pig has not been trained properly. But don't worry, if you are passionate about pig keeping, you will enjoy this aspect of piggy care.

We have tried to provide lots of practical guidance in helping you to train your pig.

6 – Pigs are Greedy

This perception is probably very accurate! Pigs do tend to be gluttonous. This means that they will eat as much as is on offer. They will usually eat until they physically vomit, and they have even been known to eat their own vomit.

You will need to follow and provide an appropriate diet and ensure your pet pig consumes all the necessary nutrients. Your Micro Pig will be healthy and happy as a result and very importantly, not obese.

7 – Pigs cannot swim

Fascinatingly, this is a misperception. Pigs are actually reasonable swimmers - and some domestic pigs seem to love swimming!

There is an Island in the Bahama's known as Pig Island. It is uninhabited by people but is the home to many pigs (sounds amazing doesn't it!).

Cruise ships circle near the Island and the pigs have come to realize that people throw scraps of food from the boat. Intelligent as we know they are, the pigs have decided that it is well worth the effort to swim out near the boats to see what food they can find.

Chapter 2 – Characteristics of Different Breeds

The Micro Pig is smaller than a farm pig, but this not does not mean it will be tiny. There is not a pig that is the size of a teacup, or one that could fit inside your pocket.

Now that we have established that the Micro Pig is not an actual breed of pig, it is interesting to look at the different types of pigs that fall into the classification of a Micro Pig.

It is worth observing that most pet pigs are not a pure breed of pig but in fact a cross breed of some variation.

Since the original breeding stock is no longer around, it is difficult to trace the true breed of these pigs – this explains why these pigs are frequently referred to as mini pigs – it is really a mix of breeds.

Origins

The Vietnamese Pot-belly pig descends from a traditional Vietnamese breed. Probably the most common type of Miniature Pig that is adopted as a pet today is derived from a cross breed of these pot-belly pigs from South East Asia.

The potbelly pigs, generally associated with South East Asia and particularly Vietnam, are technically not a breed of pigs but a local type (generally typical of a local area).

Chapter 2 – Characteristics of Different Breeds

The term **breed** means *"a stock of animals or plants within a species having a distinctive appearance and typically having been developed by deliberate selection"*.

The type and variety of potbellied pigs we see in the United States today are the result of cross-breeding four 'local types' of Vietnamese pigs. They share similar physical characteristics and originate in different parts of Vietnam.

Prior to the 1970's the traditional Vietnamese pot-belly pig was the most numerous across the area. It is estimated that numbers of this type of pig went into the millions. However, from the 1970's, another type of breed became much more dominant, the Mong Cai. This was because it was more productive.

In 1991, the total number of the Vietnamese potbelly was estimated at 675 000. By 2010, the estimated number was 120. In 2003 its conservation status was listed as critical and by 2007, as endangered.

During the 1960's, a relatively small number of the Vietnamese potbellies were exported to Sweden and Canada, to be housed in zoos or used in scientific laboratory experiments.

Over the next decade, they began to spread to animal parks throughout Europe and some were reared on smallholdings.

In the mid 1980's, Canadian Keith Connell bought the pot-bellied pigs into North America with the intention of supplying the pigs to zoos. It was actually a private buyer who became interested in these pigs as pets – and here began the love and fascination of keeping these pigs as house pets.

Soon after Connell imported these pigs to America, at least two other breed types were also introduced.

Connell's importation became known as the Con Line and their characteristics form the basis of the foundation stock.

One of the other breed types has become known as the Lea Line. These were imported by Leavitt. These pigs displayed a gentle temperament, white and black markings and were slightly smaller than the Con Line.

The other breed type introduced became known as the O'Royal Line, imported by Espberger – these were predominantly white and slightly larger in size.

These pigs – the Con Line, Lea Line and Royal Line form the basis of the pot-belly pigs we see in America today. The different lines provide a greater gene pool which enables breeders to produce a healthier breed type with desirable characteristics (things such as size, temperament, color).

This has meant that they have excellent qualities well suited for a house pet.

Size;

On average, the pigs that first arrived from Canada into North America weighed around 250lbs (100kg). This is much larger than the potbellied pigs that are so popular today but whilst this is certainly not 'mini', it is much smaller that the farm pigs that weigh between 600 and 1500lbs.

Now, the average pot-bellied pig weighs around 120 – 150lbs (50 – 70kg). Some can reach as much as 200lbs (90kg).

They are approximately 3-foot-long (91cm) and 15 inches (38cm) tall. The potbellied pig does not reach full size until approximately 5 years old.

Physical Characteristics;

As you would expect, the pot-belly pigs have a pronounced pot-belly! The sagging belly of a pregnant sow may even reach the ground.

They have heavily wrinkled skin and are covered in hair (they shed their hair once or twice a year). They have a prominent sway back. The head tends to be small with an upturned snout, small erect ears, small eyes and heavy, sagging jowls (large in comparison to the size of head). They have a straight tail with a switch at the end.

You should be able to feel the hip bone when applying pressure, but you should not be able to see the bone structure.

There are two main types of pot-bellies recognized within the breed; the I-Mo or Fatty I and the l-pha or large I.

The I-Mo is the typical short-legged pig. It has a short snout and small upward erect ears.

The l-pha has longer legs and is taller. It has a longer snout and it has bigger ears which point out horizontally.

Coloring;

The potbelly pigs are most commonly completely black with occasional white on the snout, head, feet or tail. They can also be completely white or gray.

General Temperament;

The pot-belly pig has a temperament similar to other domestic pigs. Pigs are smart animals and the pot-belly is no different – it is extremely intelligent and highly trainable. Also, very sociable and affectionate.

Since the pot-bellies have been bred to be pets as opposed to meat, they have become calmer and more loving towards their owner than other breeds of domestic pig.

Moreover, pot-bellies are usually extremely loyal to their owners in a similar way that a dog would be.

Because the pot-bellied pig is a prey animal it will be easily scared. A display of what might appear to be aggressive behavior may be explained by the fact that the pig is frightened. The potbelly is a herd animal and will need to be taught its place in the herd.

Life Expectancy

The lifespan of the average pot-belly pig is between 10 – 15 years.

Kunekune

The name is pronounced as 'cooney cooney'.

Origins;

The Kunekune are a unique New Zealand breed of pig; and it is thought that they descended from an Asian domestic breed that were bought to New Zealand. Indeed, there are no indigenous land animals in New Zealand.

There are many explanations on how they got to New Zealand. It is likely that the Kunekunes were introduced to New Zealand by either whalers or traders (possibly both) around the early 19th century from Asia.

Or perhaps the Maori's bought the Kunekunes to New Zealand from Polynesia – after all pigs were very important in Polynesian culture and there are still pigs with tassles (as with the Kunekune) on the South Pacific Islands.

It was in New Zealand that the Kunekune developed into its present state. The Maori communities of New Zealand kept the Kunekune pigs and they were, on the whole, not known about by the European settlers.

They were highly valued by the Maori people as a source of meat and fat (the fat was used to preserve food). They had a tendency not to roam and a very placid nature – qualities highly valued by the Maori people.

By the 1970's, the Maori people did not keep Kunekune pigs very much for meat anymore and numbers of these pigs saw a spectacular decline.

In 1984 Staglands Wildlife Reserve and Willowbank Wildlife Reserve collected 18 Kunekune pigs and began a captive breeding program.

This was in response to concern over a dramatic fall in numbers; the breed appeared to be facing extinction with an estimated 50 Kunekune pigs in existence. Due to this and other recovery programs, thankfully the breed is no longer facing extinction.

The majority of Kunekune pigs in New Zealand descended from those 18 pigs in the breeding program. The Kunekune pigs are now widely spread throughout New Zealand again.

In 2004, it was estimated that there were 5000 Kunekune pigs in New Zealand (both registered and unregistered). The Kunekune pigs can now be found in the United States, the United Kingdom and throughout Europe.

Because these pigs were brought back from near extinction, there are several breeders in New Zealand, the United States and the United Kingdom.

Size;

The Kunekune will grow to approximately 60 cm (24 inch) tall. This makes it one of the smallest domesticated breeds of pig.

A fully grown Kunekune can weigh between 60 and 200 kg (approx. 130lb to 440lbs). Although large, compare this to the average weight of a domestic pig which Is up to 350kg (770lbs).

The Kunekune will reach its full size at 2 – 3 years old. Whilst this is the smallest breed of pig it is worth reminding ourselves that this is still a big animal. It is much rounder and fatter than a dog.

The piglets are very tiny and as small as a teacup, they could sit in the palm of your hand – but remember that this little piglet will grow much much bigger.

Physical Characteristics;

The Kunekune pigs have a very distinctive physical appearance which is quite different to Potbelly Pigs.

They are covered in hair which can be straight, curly, long or short. It has a short to medium black snout that points upwards. The head is medium to short and the ears are either pricked or semi lopped.

The legs of the Kunekune tend to be very short and their bodies are short and round.

The shape of their body is perhaps best described by the meaning of the Polynesian word 'Kunekune' which actually means plump!

The Kunekune often have tassels hanging from their lower jaw (under their chin) – these are known as pire pire and they are about 4cm long. However not all purebreds have these tassels.

Coloring;

There are a variety of different colors; black, black and white, brown, tan, gold and white. They also come in a variety of spotty colors.

General Temperament

The Kunekune pigs tend to be very sociable, friendly, playful and easy going with an even temperament. They tend to love human company and are highly trainable.

Life Expectancy

The lifespan of a Kunekune is expected to be around 12 to 15 years.

Juliana Pig

The Juliana is also known as the Miniature Painted Pig.

Origins

The Juliana Pig is not a true breed of pig but the result of selective breeding of various kinds of pigs. It is thought to originate from Europe and its unique features are that it is small, colorful and spotted.

Indeed, it was developed through a selective breeding program to reinforce small size, temperament and intelligence.

The Juliana pig has been specifically bred to work with humans. This means that its disposition and personality is always of great importance when considering breeding. Breeders strive to produce offspring that display the same temperament and characteristics as the original Juliana Pig.

The Juliana breed is quite an old one, but it is not known whether the modern Juliana Pigs are of the same ancestry. However, the modern Juliana closely resembles the original Juliana and perhaps more so than any other breed of pig.

Size

On average, a Juliana Pig weighs between 30 pounds (14 kg) to 50 pounds (23 kg).

In general, the Juliana Pig measures between 15 inches (38 cm) and 17 inches (43 cm) in height.

No Juliana Pig should be over 65 pounds (30kg) when fully mature.

Physical Characteristics

The physical characteristics of the Juliana Pig are more similar to a domestic or feral pig than a pot-bellied pig. Indeed, it should not display a pot-belly; it should be lean and longer than it is tall. It should not be plump or heavily wrinkled.

The Juliana Pig has a long and straight snout. The eyes tend to be clearly visible and range from blue to virtually black. Ears are small and erect.

The body of the Juliana pig tends to be muscular and lean. The top line should be straight and of a good length. Chest and shoulders should be medium width (in other words not broad or narrow). It is acceptable for there to be a slight sway in the back, but this tends to be discouraged. The tummy should be firm with no potbelly.

The tail of the Juliana Pig is straight when relaxed. When the pig is excited or moving, the tail can become curled or twisted.

The hair of the Juliana is thick and coarse. It may even be quite long in the winter. The spots may fade or blend in when the hair is longer but the pigmentation on the skin should be visible when washed or shaved.

Coloring

The Juliana Pig is always spotted. Its base color ranges from silver, white, red, rust, black and cream. Spots are normally black but can also be red or white. There should be an abundance of spots and the spots should be random (not in a piebald or mottled pattern).

General Temperament

The temperament of the Juliana is one of the best attributes of this breed. Perhaps because they have been bred with a focus on their personality traits.

Their characteristics can be regarded as similar to that of a dog. They tend to be relaxed and laid back, easy going and good companions to other animals and people.

Life Expectancy

The Juliana pig has a lifespan averaging 14 to 18 years of age.

American Guinea Hog
(African Pygmy)

Also known as the Pineywoods Guinea, Guinea Forest Hog, Acorn Eater and Yard Pig.

Guinea Hogs are naturally larger and arguably not a Micro Pig. However, I have decided to include this breed as they are frequently referred to as a Mini Pig.

Although the Guinea Hog is smaller than industrial hog breeds, its' moderate size means that it is still primarily used on small scale farms for its lard and meat.

By Drew Avery (Guinea Hog {suinae sus}) [CC BY 2.0 (http://creativecommons.org/licenses/by/2.0)], via Wikimedia Commons

Also note that the American Guinea Hog tends to be more popular with homesteads due to its love for foraging and grazing.

They thrive where ranging and grazing is a constant activity. Their slightly larger size and requirements for grazing mean that they probably make less suitable house pets than other types of mini pigs.

Origins

It is believed that the Guinea Hog originated on the Guinea Coast of Africa. Due largely to the slave trade, the Guinea Hog spread to United Kingdom, France, Spain and United States of America.

They were very popular in Southern USA, frequently seen on homesteads. During the late 19th and early 20th century, most households in America cooked with lard – the Guinea Hog produced this abundantly.

As the popularity of lard declined, the numbers of American Guinea Hog numbers also diminished dramatically.

At that time, the true African Guinea Hogs were large and of a squarish shape. They had bristly hair that was reddish. Their ears were pointed, and they had a long tail. They were grazers and foragers but could still be used for pork and lard.

The original strain, despite being virtually black, displayed hints of red. This led to the name 'Red Guineas'. Despite being so popular at the beginning of the 19th century, this strain is now extinct.

Later these pigs were crossed with other breeds, including Appalachian English Pigs, Essex Pigs and West African Dwarfs. This new breed is now generally known as the American Guinea Hog and is regarded as a true American heritage breed of domestic farm pig, arguably over 200 years old.

It has retained its black coloring, but the hint of red has disappeared. Consequently, it is now sometimes called the Black Guinea.

By the end of the 19th century, this breed had too seen a dramatic decline and were in danger of becoming extinct.

In 2005, the American Guinea Hog Association was formed. This organization is dedicated to ensuring the continued existence of the Guinea Hog.

Size

Now Guinea Hogs are much smaller – approximately 150 pounds (70 kg) – 300 pounds (140 kg). It is easy to fatten the

American Guinea Hogs so it is very important not to overfeed.

In general, they measure 22 inches (56 cm) – 27 inches (70 cm) tall.

Males are usually one or two inches taller than females.

Physical Characteristics

American Guinea Hogs have small to medium sized ears which are upright (sometimes slightly bent at the tip). Their snouts can vary from short to medium-long. The tail has a single curl. Eyes often face slightly forward.

They tend to have medium to long hair which is coarse, bristly and black (some tinged in red - brown tones and some blue - black tones).

Coloring

Today the Guinea Hogs are normally black. A common anomaly is solid black with minimal white points at the feet and tip of the nose. Excess white (beyond the feet and end of the snout) tends to be discouraged.

General Temperament

They are very placid, even tempered and gentle in nature, making them easy to look after. The females display exceptional mothering skills. As a result of their good nature, they have become very popular in children's zoos.

Life Expectancy

The life span of the American Guinea Hog is between 10 and 15 years.

Ossabaw Island Pig

By Tim Evanson [CC BY-SA 2.0 (https://creativecommons.org/licenses/by-sa/2.0)], via Wikimedia Commons

This is a rarely available breed of a Micro Pig. There are small breeding groups of Ossabaw Island pigs (descendants of the Ossabaw Island Pigs brought from the Island to the mainland in the 1970's). Offspring from these are occasionally available from individual breeders.

Although a breeding population has been established on American farms on the mainland, they do remain a critically endangered variety of pig.

Origins

Ossabaw Island is off the coast of Georgia and the Ossabaw Island Pigs originated from Spanish pigs that were bought to North America over 400 years ago.

These pigs were small in size, with long snouts, heavy coats and prick ears. Over time, these Spanish pigs escaped and became feral. Inevitably they mixed with other domestic pigs. However, uniquely, the pigs on the Island of Ossabaw were an isolated population and so have remained much closer to their origins.

The poor supply of food on the Island meant that these pigs had a more restricted diet. Consequently, over time, they became smaller.

This is a process caller insular dwarfism. Their diet also meant that they developed an unusual biochemical system of fat metabolism. This means that they store more fat than any other variety of pig. They also have a form of low grade, non-insulin dependent diabetes. This has made them very useful as animals in medical research.

Quarantine restrictions mean that it is illegal to import these pigs directly from Ossabaw Island.

Size

In their natural environment, the Ossabaw Island Pigs tend to be very small – a sow that is pregnant can weigh as little as 100lbs. In captivity and as pets, these pigs tend to grow much larger.

At full maturity, the Ossabaw Island Pig tends to reach around 200 pounds (90 kg). On average, height will be approximately 20 inches (50 cm).

Physical Characteristics

The Ossabaw Island Pig has a long narrow snout that is designed for rooting. It has ears that are erect and forward facing. The head is heavily built and slightly dished.

The body shape is rather rectangular. Legs are short and straight with toes facing forward. They are covered in thick bristly fur.

Coloring

The Ossabaw Island Pig has a wide range of color variations. Colors include black, spotted black and white, red and tan. The most common coloring is black.

General Temperament

Very intelligent, clean and with a friendly nature.

Life Expectancy

The average life expectancy of the Ossabaw Island Pig is between 10 and 15 years.

Chapter 3 – So Why Keep a Pet Pig?

The popularity of the Mini Pig has exploded over the past few years. We have seen celebrities adopting pigs as pets and there have also been YouTube pig celebrities.

Media has shown us that many pet pigs are left homeless and in need of rescue. Sanctuaries have become established to address this crisis but it is often reported that they are unable to meet demand.

So how about we put an end to the 'craze'? Not in the sense that nobody should keep a pet pig – more that this should be a highly considered pet and people should recognize that it will put a lot of demands on you and your family.

In a similar way to our treatment of dogs, 'a dog is for life not just for Christmas', let's give this wonderful animal and could be pet a chance. Find out as much as you can and reflect on whether this is something you will want for the next 15 years or so.

There is no reason that pigs should not be accepted as pets. However, if you are not adequately prepared, you will sadly be unable to meet the needs of your new pet. So be prepared and be a fantastic owner.

Chapter 3 – So Why Keep a Pet Pig?

In the United States, pigs are regarded as exotic pets. The 'exotic' status originates from their high regard in Chinese and Asian cultures – here pigs have been kept as pets for centuries.

There are zoning laws which control where they can be kept. This is because pigs are identified by the law as swine animals that are kept for producing meat. Swine are kept in herds that can be dense. This makes it easy for disease to spread.

Mini pigs are undoubtedly demanding pets. They are incredibly intelligent and very social. Their size means that they require adaptations in terms of being kept as a pet inside the home.

We have seen that the mini pigs are only miniature as a basis for comparison to the pigs developed to produce food. Pet pigs do not have the same needs and should not be treated the same as a pig that has been bred for the intention of production.

To assist you in deciding whether a pig may be the pet for you, let's explore the Advantages and Disadvantages.

Advantages

Highly Trainable

Pigs are extremely intelligent animals and this quality makes them highly trainable. In a similar way to intelligent dog breeds, they can follow instructions and learn performance tricks. They can even be toilet trained so that they can live indoors.

A pig is so attached to food that this can be used as a positive way to train your pet pig. Pigs are always so determined to do anything for food and have a mental capacity to understand a reward system. This means that they are very enthusiastic to learn and respond remarkably well to training.

The brain of a pig is very highly developed, following in rank just behind a dolphin. This means that like the dolphin, the pig is very socially dependent, very sophisticated in communication and expression.

Devoted and Loyal

Pigs are incredibly sociable animals and really hunger for company and close companionship. Being herd animals, they are affectionate to other members of the herd. Therefore, they often make excellent companions to individuals and families.

As they are used to living in a herd, they seem to really enjoy and thrive on the warmth and closeness of a pack. This means they will like cuddling up on the sofa, in a blanket or even in bed with you if you like.

Chapter 3 – So Why Keep a Pet Pig?

Communicative

Pigs have very sophisticated communication skills.

In addition to squealing, pigs bark, cough and even seem to laugh. Like dogs, pigs will bark when feeling under threat or when detecting signs of danger.

When excited, perhaps to say hello or when expecting something good to happen, a pig seems to squeal with laughter and displays a wide variation of different squeals.

You will be able to differentiate between the sounds your pig makes so that can understand how your pet is feeling. This tends to create a close bond between pet and owner.

Instinctively Inquisitive

When a pig is not engrossed in eating or socializing, they will instinctively put snout to the ground to explore.

Rooting is a natural way of exploring. Pigs have extremely poor eyesight which means that they rely on smell and their memory to find their way around. Pigs have such an immense sense of smell that they can smell something that it buried 25 feet (7.6 meter) under the ground.

With excellent memories, the pig will use its' nose to find out about where they are – they will then be able to run around without bumping into anything.

This is because the pig has found out about its' environment through smell and is then able to retain that information in detail.

Naturally Squeaky Clean!

Pigs are surprisingly clean and do not have an odor. Unlike cats, pigs do not bring home dead animals. They also do not roll in their own poop. Toileting wise, they can easily be house trained.

Easy Everyday Maintenance

You will be very busy addressing the social needs of your pig, but he / she does not require much in terms of physical maintenance.

All being well, your mini pig will only need to see the vet once yearly. This is for regular vaccinations and hoof trimming. So ordinarily, you will not have expensive vet bills. Routine care can become more challenging and expensive if the mini pig experiences health difficulties.

Hypoallergenic

The hair of a bristly pig is hypoallergenic. As pigs have hair instead of fur, they may make an excellent alternative pet for people allergic to fur.

Disadvantages

Manipulative Without Question

With their high level of intelligence, pigs do have the ability to be very manipulative. Combine this intelligence with their obsession for food; they now have the ultimate motivation to exploit your goodwill.

They will literally do anything for food. They can identify weak spots in their owners and will unhesitatingly use this to their advantage.

The same strength and quality that makes them easily and highly trainable also makes them quite devious. They are opportunists and unrelenting in their desire for food.

Pigs can recognize and make the most of the tricks that benefit them the most.

They will very happily learn how to sit and perform tricks with the reward of food.

Equally, they will happily learn how to open the fridge, cupboards and any door that stands between themselves and food.

Destructive Tendencies

Pigs can be undeniably destructive. Without adequate attention and consistent roles, destructive and even ruinous behavior will be inevitable. Pigs that are bored and feel neglected are the most destructive.

A bored pig that begins rooting around your home may end up tearing up carpets and flooring. They will tip plant pots upside down to sniff through the dirt. They will eat drywall.

Interaction with your pig and lots of attention will avoid this but you need to be able to make this commitment for the following 15 years.

Finding a place in the Herd

As pigs are instinctively herd animals. They will automatically search for their place within it. The pig will need to identify a leader of the herd.

Without that, the pig will attempt to assert themselves as head of the herd. A pig that regards itself as head of the herd is likely to display more aggressive behavior.

This can include charging at children or strangers, especially if there is food involved.

Messy Housemates

Although the pig itself will be clean and tidy, expect your outdoor space to be messy or indeed, 'higgledy piggledy'! A pig will instinctively root around when it is not eating or interacting with you.

Rooting is very natural behavior and a pig needs to be able to root. It is their way of exploring their surroundings in addition to searching for food.

Through rooting, they find vitamins and minerals from the ground and will eat anything from acorns to worms. This instinctive need to root is unavoidably chaotic and untidy.

The solution to this problem must be acceptance on your part – if you are able to tolerate the mess in your outside space then consider this problem solved.

However, if you do value a neat and tidy outdoor space then you may need to reconsider having a pig as a pet.

High Heat Sensitivity

Pigs are quite vulnerable to overheating. They are not able to sweat and during hot weather; pigs need to lower their body temperature so that they do not overheat. They will require a 'mud hole' or kiddy pool so that they can stay cool.

Health Problems and Stress

As with all pets, pigs come with their own unique health issues. They are not built to withstand any kind of physical exertion and can suffer with stress and are susceptible to overheating.

In comparison to its' large stomach, the pig has very small lungs. In part due to its' inactive lifestyle, pigs often suffer with lung infections. Stress or challenging weather conditions can lead to pneumonia which can kill a pig very suddenly.

Pigs really enjoy a calm and relaxed lifestyle with weather that is not in either extreme.

Chapter 4 - What all Piggy Parents Must Know

Mini pigs are undeniably a fantastic choice of pet for devoted owners.

However, be sure that you are completely prepared; there are some additional practical considerations that you will need to make, including laws that you must be aware of.

Zoning Laws

Did you know that it may not be legal to keep a pig as a pet?

According to law set by the United States Department of Agriculture and the majority of City Governments, pigs fall into the legal category of livestock.

This means that you are obliged to check with City Government Regulations before bringing a Mini Pig into your home as a pet.

Zoning Laws are intended to prevent the spread of disease amongst livestock. The regulations are designed to protect both animal and people.

Chapter 4 - What all Piggy Parents Must Know

Pigs are categorized by the law as swine animals that are kept for producing meat. Because swine are kept in herds, sometimes very large, disease can spread easily and very quickly.

There are many cities which do not allow pet pigs to live with the boundaries of the city. Some cities allow pigs but have restrictions in place. Examples include only one pig per household, compulsory vaccinations, weight restrictions.

There is not a list of cities and towns which are zoned or not. You will need to go to your local Zoning Department and check. Sometimes you can do this online otherwise contact by phone or in person.

If you discover that you cannot legally keep a pet pig where you live, do still contact your Local City Government.

There is a chance that you may be able to have the regulation changed or updated. Contact your City Council and find out if there is any possibility of an update or change to your Zoning Laws. Some City Governments have been prepared to make amendments and some have not.

It is imperative that you contact your Local City Government Offices before you go ahead and adopt or buy your new pet pig.

Many pet pigs have been surrendered to Animal Sanctuaries because owners have bought a pet pig and then realized that it is illegal in the place where they live.

Zoning Restrictions are one of the main reasons why pigs end up unwanted. It is unrealistic to think that you will be able to hide your pet pig. Somebody will report it and your pig will be taken away from you.

Rental Properties and Homeowners Associations

Landlords and Homeowner Associations may place legal restrictions on whether you can keep a pet pig in your property. There have been many reports on legal battles where families have been told that they are unable to keep their pet pig, or they will no longer be able to live in their home.

Avoid facing homelessness or having to part with your new pet; research first on whether your Homeowner Association or Landlords allow pigs as pets.

Suitable Micro Pig Veterinarians

Locating a veterinarian in your local area that will treat and care for Micro Pigs can be an obstacle for some people. There are surprisingly few Veterinary Clinics that will treat Micro Pigs.

Contact your local vets and enquire.

If your vet does not treat Micro Pets, they may be able to refer you to another vet. Consider asking your breeder, sanctuary, another owner of a Micro Pig or any Pig communities that you may be associated with.

Find out whether the vet you are considering registering with has a specialty or sub-specialty with pigs / swine. Ask how much experience your prospective vet has had with treating and looking after pigs.

You will need to ensure you have the means to transport your pig to the Veterinarian Clinic. This will probably include a harness and a crate.

It is imperative that you find a suitable vet for your pig before a medical emergency arises. Once you have bought your pet pig home, it will be valuable to arrange an appointment with the vet you intend to use.

Travelling with your Pet Pig
Although you may not plan on taking your Mini Pig in the car on a regular basis, car journeys to the vets will be unavoidable. Consequently, familiarize your pig with car journeys and make sure that it is comfortable and not

stressful. This will help with standard vet check-ups and will be critical for emergency trips for medical help.

Initially, just take your pig with you on short drives so that they can become used to the car. It may be that your pig enjoys accompanying you on car journeys and it could become part of your everyday routine.

However, it should be noted that not all pigs will enjoy it and some may feel frightened by the experience. If you have a young pig, it may be worth trying a few car rides early on. This may help your pig cope better with car rides as it becomes older – it has the experience to know that car rides are not threatening.

You will need a crate for car journeys as this is the only safe way for your pig to travel.

Transporting a pig in the back of the trunk or pickup truck would be unsafe, likewise allowing the pig to move freely around a moving vehicle would also be unsafe.

Provide your pet with the opportunity to familiarize itself with the crate beforehand so that the pig is not scared of the crate. Indeed, allow your pig to know that the crate is a place where they can feel safe.

Keep the crate on the back seat or at the back of the vehicle. Note that the crate should be large enough that your pig can stand up and turn around.

It is unquestionably not safe for you or your pig to travel without a crate. Cute as it may seem, do not let your pig sit next to you in the car. This can lead to a dangerous situation.

Note that some veterinarians will not see the pig unless it is in a crate or kennel.

Also, you need to be aware of high temperatures on car journeys. We have seen that pigs can suffer with health problems if they overheat.

Switch on the air conditioning whenever you think it may not be cool enough for your pig. Remember that the back of the car (where your pig should be) will generally be warmer than at the front where you are sitting.

In addition, consider making the journey at night if the daytime temperatures are high. Ensure that your Micro Pig has plenty to drink. You can also place a wet towel underneath your pig to try and keep him / her cool.

Another option is to cover the windows with car window shades to reduce the amount of direct sunlight coming into the car.

Travel – Laws and Regulations

When you are going to be travelling out of state with your Micro Pig, there are Laws and Regulations that you need to know. It is essential that you check with the United States Department of Agriculture within your state as well as the states you are going to or simply travelling through.

Each state has different regulations for entering and leaving with swine (which as we know is what the USDA categorizes mini pigs as). The regulations exist to prevent the spread of disease.

Certain states require a recent and up to date Health Certificate. Others will require blood tests. Typically, these are valid for 30 dates from the date of issue but check this with each state you are travelling within.

Pigs Love Being Outside

Irrespective of their size and whether you have enough room inside, pigs love to be outside. They have a natural instinct to root, dig, forage and explore with their snouts. As pigs have poor eyesight, this behavior is imperative so your pig can find out about their surroundings and where they live.

Rooting in the ground also enables the pig to search for food. Indeed, by rooting in the dirt, your pig will find and benefit from essential nutrients.

Providing a safe, secure and pig proof outdoor area is essential.

Chapter 4 - What all Piggy Parents Must Know

In the wild, a pig will spend the majority of the day rooting around in the ground in search of food.

When a pig is kept indoors, this natural and instinctive behavior is still just as important to your pet.

If a pig is not able to root around in the garden, they will certainly display much more destructive behavior indoors where the pig will try and root up the carpet, floorboards, sofa and more.

Consider where you live and whether you have appropriate and adequate outdoor space to keep your Micro Pig happy and healthy.

Chapter 5 – Estimated Costs

The Mini Pig has many additional demands to a more traditional pet. This can include financial demands.

To help prepare you, here is an outline of some of the estimated costs of owning a Micro Pig.

Estimating the monthly costs of owning your pig is equally important as knowing that you have the time and motivation to feed the pig and look after its' basic needs. Remember that in addition to the initial outset, there are ongoing costs of care.

Adopting or Buying

Choosing between buying from a breeder and adopting from a Sanctuary is a very personal decision.

There are many pigs in Sanctuaries in desperate need of a home and you will be doing a wonderful thing by adopting.

You will be providing a pig with a second chance, loving owners and new home.

Pigs find themselves in Animal Shelters for a wide variety of reasons.

Some of these pigs have been well cared for by their previous owner. Other pigs have had a very difficult life, have experienced neglect and have not had their needs met.

Pigs who have had a difficult past will need specialist care from their new owner. Ideally, an experienced owner may be well suited to adopting a pig lacking socialization or a behaviorally challenging pig.

A first-time pig owner would be better to adopt a pig that came from a home where it was previously well cared for. It may already be socialized, trained and already familiar with car rides, baths and harnesses.

Shelters tend to work hard to match up pigs to a suitable owner. This explains why you will be asked lots of questions by the Rescue Centre. It is not intended as an invasion of your privacy but more as the best way to match up a pig to the best suited owner.

If you decide to adopt your Mini Pig from a shelter, one of your initial expenses will be the adoption fee. This cost is considerably less than buying a pig from a breeder.

The majority of Rescue Centers are not for profit organizations and so charge very nominal adoption fees. You can expect to pay approximately $100 for fully mature pigs and $150 for piglets. This is only a guide and will vary amongst different Animal Shelters.

However, if you are interested in a purebred then you will need to go through a breeder. When searching for pig breeders, you will discover that there are various breeders who charge different rates.

Costs tend to range between $600 to $1000. Breeders typically charge an additional deposit rate which will be between $100 and $250.

Established and reputable pig breeders should provide you with registration documents, vaccination records and will often spay or neuter the pig. They also spend time with the

pigs, helping to train and socialize them. This will make for a much easier transition when it is time for you to bring your new piggy addition to your family home.

It is of utmost importance that you purchase your Micro Pig from a reliable breeder.

There have been a lot of people who have purchased piglets that they thought would be Mini that have actually turned out to be full-grown farm sized pigs.

Use the internet to search for registered breeders. These breeders have registered their breeding pigs and have agreed to follow a code of ethics. They can provide proof of age plus photographic documentation of the measurements of their pigs.

Costs of Spaying and Neutering

Pigs that have not been spayed or neutered do not make easy or enjoyable pets.

Chapter 5 – Estimated Costs

Without spaying or neutering your pig, you can expect to see odor and behavioral problems. It is also important to note that pigs can breed as early as 3 months old.

This explains why spaying and neutering is an additional and substantial cost that must be accounted for.

Both pigs adopted through Shelters and from reputable breeders will often have already been spayed or neutered.

Sometimes this will be an additional cost that you will be charged and sometimes it is included in the price of your pig. It is vital that you check, and it is also worth checking documents for proof that it has been done.

Spaying or neutering usually costs between $300 to $500.

Everyday Living Expenses
Care and feeding a Miniature Pig will generally cost between $20 to $60 per month. This will vary on the size of the pig as this affects how much food they will require.

As well as the cost of food, you may be advised by your vet that your pig will benefit from vitamin supplements.

In addition to the cost of feeding your pig, you will need to consider housing, fencing and bedding costs.

Bedding can be expensive but your Micro Pig will appreciate it and depend on it for its' warmth and comfort.

Be aware that your pig will be so fond of eating that he / she may even eat their bedding, whether this be straw or a knitted blanket. On a farm, the most commonly used bedding for a pig would be straw, sawdust, or untreated wood shavings.

Medical Costs

Veterinary costs are very unpredictable because they ultimately depend on the health and well-being of your pig. Some illnesses and problems are unavoidable and will need medical attention from your vet.

Veterinary bills will include vaccinations, parasite treatments, tusk or hoof trims, treatments for injuries, illnesses plus general check-ups. Indeed, regular hoof care is essential for pigs to prevent future problems with their legs.

Owners should expect to pay between $100 and $300 a year on regular medical expenses. This does not include any unexpected health problems.

Additional Costs

There are many items that you will need to purchase before you bring home your beloved Micro Pig.

The majority of these will be a one-off purchase. Have a look at Chapter 8 'Becoming Piggy Prepared'. There is a section on '**Getting Ready**' which is essentially a check list of items that you will need to buy. These are all expenses you will need to consider when working out the estimated costs.

There is the additional cost of damage that your Mini Pig may do to your home. Throughout the 15 years of their life, your beloved Mini Pig is very likely to cause some damage or destruction to your home. This inevitably will mean replacing some of your possessions.

Another major expense is paying for care while you are away on vacation or for any other reason. The cost of this varies depending on whether you have a close friend or family member who can help, or you choose a kennel or a pet sitter. Refer to 'Chapter 6 – Before you Adopt or Buy' and look at the section '**Care while you are Away**'.

Chapter 6 – Before you Adopt or Buy

Choosing a Rescue Organization

It may be that you have decided that you would like to adopt / rescue your Mini Pig.

Your next step will be to select a Rescue Organization that you have full confidence in. It will be helpful if you know exactly what to expect from a high quality and reputable Rescue Center.

Rescue Homes should provide excellent veterinary care for all their Mini Pigs. Indeed, every pig should be up to date on vaccines, be dewormed and microchipped.

All Mini Pigs must be spayed or neutered before going to their new homes. This is very important as this protects the pig. Also without it, the pig would not make a suitable pet.

Every single medical condition that a pig has should be dealt with before the pig is ready to be adopted. Veterinarians will assess and treat any pig as soon as there is a sign of illness or injury.

Chapter 6 – Before you Adopt or Buy

A good Rescue Home should ask you lots of questions! They will screen all prospective families interested in adopting. This will include a foster / adoption application, veterinary reference, phone interview and a home visit.

The purpose of this screening process is to protect the pigs from being placed in a home where it may experience abuse or neglect.

It is the responsibility of the Rescue Home to ensure that the Mini Pigs are going to suitable homes and owners who will look after them well. You should not consider that you are being judged but more that the Rescue Center needs to absolutely sure for the sake of the Mini Pig.

A reputable Rescue Shelter will document the adoption process. This is to protect the pig and the Rescue Organization. Each pig will have a permanent record that will include a surrender form, adoption application, adoption contract, foster application and foster contracts.

The Rescue Center will be knowledgeable of and follow all State Laws regarding travel including permanent identification, CVI or Health Certificates, vaccines and / or bloodwork depending on what is required by Law.

A Rescue Organization will be able to support you in selected the right pig for you.

They understand the pigs that they have in their care and can help select a pig that would fit in well with your family and home situation.

The only motivation of the Rescue Center is to find a suitable home for the Mini Pig.

Note that the Rescue Center may not know the full history of the pig you are considering adopting. The vet may have to make an approximate estimation of how old the pig is.

As well as Rescue Organizations, you will be able to find details of pigs needing homes just by looking online.

The Pig Placement Network is a fantastic place to start (pigplacementnetwork.org). They work with animal shelters, humane societies and pet pig owners to rescue unwanted, abused or abandoned pet pigs and find a place for them in a loving new home.

There are also pigs in Craigslist, pigs posted in groups on Facebook and other dedicated pages. You will find that there is an abundance of pigs needing a new home.

Adopting from an individual is not regulated and so every experience is different.

Chapter 6 – Before you Adopt or Buy

Be aware that if you are unable to keep the pig for any reason, it is very probable that the previous owner will not take the pig back.

This is different to an Animal Sanctuary where they would automatically accept the pig back if things didn't work out. Ask as many questions you can think of and consider contacting the veterinarian who treats the pig.

Finding the Right Breeder

If you have chosen to purchase your Micro Pig from a breeder, ask as many questions as you can to be sure that you have found a good breeder.

A good breeder should be well-informed and happy to provide you with as much information as you need. They should allow you to visit on site. You will want to see the parents and the living environment of your prospective piglet.

If you are unable to visit as you live too far away, your breeder should provide you with current photographs / videos.

Ask your breeder for references from previous customers, and a veterinarian.

You may like to ask the breeder for the ages of the pig's parents. Pigs can breed from as young as 3 months and do not reach their full size until they are around 3 years old. It is possible for a breeder to show you the parents and not mention that the parents are not yet at their full size. So, if you are trying to estimate the size of your piglet from looking at the parents, be sure to find out if the parents are at their fully-grown size.

Also remember that the size of the parents is only part of the picture when predicting the size of your piglet – it does not guarantee anything; offspring can always be larger!

Ask the breeder how old the piglet will be when coming home with you. There are different viewpoints on the precise 'correct age' but you want to be certain that the piglet is old enough to be weaned from his / her Mother.

Many people regard 8 weeks to be the minimum age, and before this time they should be socialized and with their litter and their mum.

The breeder should have a policy which means that will take any Mini Pig back or assist with re-homing regardless of situation – reputable breeders will take the Mini Pig back and then find another new home for them.

A breeder who is responsible will want to stay in touch to hear feedback about the piglet. They will become a source of information while you are new to piggy parenting.

Spotting Signs of a Healthy Pig

It can be an overwhelming moment when it is finally time to select the Mini Pig that will come home with you. Ensure that you take the time to notice signs of a healthy pig or piglet.

The Mini Pig should be active, alert and appear to be healthy with no sign of illness.

Eyes should be open and clear and free of discharge or crust. Mini pigs should be well rounded with no protruding bones. The pig should have solid bowel movements and be urinating appropriately. They should be clean and free of odor (they may smell however if they have been travelling in a crate due to a long journey).

The pig should have hair that looks healthy. Skin should be smooth and should not display rashes, irritations, bumps, scaling or bald patches.

The Mini Pig should look proportional and with no deformity. They should have a steady gait. They should have a straight tail. You should expect the pig to be friendly and not frightened of human contact.

Ensure that piglets are eating solid food before going home with you – to demonstrate that they are completely weaned from their mum.

Male or Female?

Choosing between a male or female Mini Pig is really a matter of personal preference. Both can make fantastic pets.

There are more differences between male and female Micro Pigs that have not been spayed or neutered. Have a look at '**Chapter 15 Piggy Healthcare'** and see the section on '**Health Benefits of Sterilizing'** where we discuss the problems of leaving pigs unaltered.

By having your pet pigs spayed or neutered, you are eliminating common problems with both male and female Micro Pigs.

Male Micro Pigs tend to be relaxed with an easy-going temperament. Female Micro Pigs are usually slightly more active than the males.

Differences between the two genders are very minimal once they have been spayed or neutered.

Indeed, much more important is how much interaction you have with your pig – this will affect their behavior much more.

Care While you are Away

Arranging care for your Mini Pig while you are on vacation can be tricky to source.

It is much more complicated than a more traditional pet. You can often ask a neighbor to call in to your house to feed a cat and there is an abundance of kennels available for dogs.

If you are not planning to go away now, don't overlook this as an issue – you will have your pet pig for a period of 10 – 15 years and it is very likely that you will want or must be away during some of this time.

There are very few (if any) kennels designed for piggy care. Occasionally dog kennels will accept pigs. However, do make certain that the dogs and pigs are kept separately.

Otherwise your piggy will have a very stressful time surrounded by predators.

Also, be sure to see where your pig will be kept at the kennels. Look at the flooring – a Mini Pig should not be kept on concrete flooring; remember its' instinctive desire to root in the dirt.

Not all pigs are well suited to kennels. Some pigs feel threatened being away from their home environment and so will experience a degree of stress.

Personality is something you need to consider. A Miniature Pig that tends to be relaxed with strangers and really enjoys socializing may be able to settle into a kennel environment. In contrast, a nervous pig that is uncomfortable around strangers is very unlikely to settle at all well.

Otherwise, you may like to consider a pet sitter.

Ensure that the pet sitter has had some experience in looking after pigs. Find out how long they will be spending with your Micro Pig. Average visit times are often around 30 minutes. You may feel that your pig will need longer if they are very keen on human company.

You may not be ready to book up this kind of care yet, but do contact pet sitters and kennels. Find out whether they can cater to the needs of a Mini Pig and investigate the costs.

Chapter 7 – One Pig or Two?

Pigs are herd animals and so are naturally very sociable. Pigs really do like other pigs and they relish in their social interactions together.

Pigs living as a herd is the most natural way for a pig and pet pigs will undoubtedly enjoy living as a pair.

However, keeping more than one pig will change the dynamics of the family and is certainly more challenging for the human owner. Indeed, you will need to work even harder to establish your dominance as the leader of the herd.

Chapter 7 – One Pig or Two?

Keeping an 'Only Pig'

Pigs have such complex and unique needs as we outline in this book.

This may make you feel that you are better able to manage one pig. Behavior can be tricky, and you may prefer to focus your attention on training one pig.

Just like it can be with children; you can be busy with one pig and as you turn around, you find that your other little treasure has been up to all sorts of mischief!

Most important of all is the fact that pigs love company and thrive on social interactions. If you are in a position to spend a lot of time with your pig on a regular basis, then your pig will be a very happy 'only pig'.

With two pigs in your home, you may notice problems with space. Mini Pigs are large animals and so naturally require a lot of room to roam around in, plus areas to sleep and rest. You will need to ensure that you can fit two pigs in your car – or else be prepared to take your pigs to the vet or other journeys on separate trips.

Remember to consider the fact that day to day living expenses will double. This of course also applies to medical expenses.

Chapter 7 – One Pig or Two?

Pigs can occasionally cause some degree of destruction in your home. The chances as well as frequency of this doubles when you have two Mini Pigs.

Having one or two pigs can feel like a very difficult decision to make.

However, providing you can meet the needs of the pig, your pig(s) will have very happy and fulfilled lives either living as one or two. Simply be honest with yourself and ask yourself whether you feel you could manage two pigs – double trouble! Think about the space in your home and whether could afford double the expense.

Pigs are such social animals that they will adapt themselves, using you and your family as their companions – or other pets as their companions. We have devoted a whole chapter to this – '**Chapter 11 - Introducing the Micro Pig to your Herd'.**

Double Trouble

Because pigs are such social creatures, they enjoy social interaction and lots and lots of it!

If you are unable to spend so much time with your pig on a regular basis, you may want to consider two pigs so that they can keep each other company.

Pigs do tend to get on very well together and so make excellent companions. Indeed, it may be that they will bond with the other pig and treat you a little less like a pig!

Chapter 7 – One Pig or Two?

Your pigs will really enjoy sleeping together. This is especially relevant if you live in a cooler climate (although pigs seem to really like cuddling up even when the weather is warmer).

Where pigs live in a larger herd, they tend to sleep in a pile together. It seems to provide something more than just warmth – perhaps fulfilling an emotional need.

So perhaps you have decided that space in your home is not an issue for you - and you have the finances to cover the cost of two pigs.

There are some additional considerations you still to make. You now have two pigs that you will need to assert your dominance over.

Also, you have the additional complexity of the interactions between the two pigs – importantly without preparation and strategies to manage behavior, it may be that your two pigs end up fighting.

Let's explore how you can ensure your pigs live in harmony together and additionally with you and your family unit.

Chapter 7 – One Pig or Two?

Pigs Living in Harmony

In an ideal situation, it is best to get two pigs at the same time and probably as young piglets. Preferably two pigs from the same litter.

This way the pigs will establish who is in charge when they are piglets. As they get older, because their place in the pecking order is already set in place, the pigs tend to get on very well with one another and it is very unusual for them to fight. This is because there is no need to fight for dominance.

Pigs of different genders can live very happily together.

Be certain that both pigs are either spayed or neutered. An unaltered pig always displays much more aggressive behavior. Pigs that have been spayed or neutered really seem to get along better and bond much quicker. In contrast, those that have not are much more likely to be aggressive and fight.

Chapter 7 – One Pig or Two?

Welcoming a Second Pig to the Family Herd

Understandably, it is not always possible to get two pigs at the same time. It might be that you start with one and as your confidence builds you may feel you are ready for another Mini Pig. This is fine but there are some additional issues to contemplate.

When looking for an additional pig, the most important consideration will be size.

Ensure that the pigs are close in size. This will mean that the pigs can defend themselves from each other and should consequently discourage fighting between them.

If your new pig is a piglet, you will need to wait until he / she is a similar size before even anticipating an introduction between the pair. The larger pig can become aggressive when displaying its' dominance over the smaller pig. It could potentially put the health and well-being of the smaller pig (or piglet) at risk.

Pigs are territorial animals and so it is difficult for them to accept another pig into their living space. If your pig is not aggressive, it may help that the 'new' pig is younger. This is because pigs do not naturally pick fights with younger members of the herd.

Chapter 7 – One Pig or Two?

If you already have a pig that seems to be quite aggressive, a second pig can actually help the situation. If the second pig is slightly larger but less aggressive, the second 'newer' pig will become the dominant one. This will likely encourage the original pig to be less aggressive.

Fighting

As soon as the pigs see each for the first time, the fighting behavior to establish dominance will begin.

You will notice that they foam at the mouth, smack their jaws, put themselves in a fighting pose – this is all normal behavior and you can allow this to happen.

Most fighting between the pigs will result in a few scratches that can easily be treated. It is their way of testing each other and establishing who is the dominant pig.

Do not introduce pigs if either has tusks as this could result in a much more serious injury, such as ripped ear or lip – this would need treatment by a veterinarian.

Chapter 7 – One Pig or Two?

After fighting and once the dominant pig has been established, the pigs usually become friends and accept each other.

Managing Acceptance

Once your pigs have accepted one another and worked out which one is dominant and which one submissive, behavior between them will be friendly and they will enjoy each other's company.

There are further strategies that you can use to help the pigs get used to each other and eventually bond.

Extremely importantly, stay and observe the pigs. They are strong animals and any fence or gate between them can be knocked down or jumped over. You are in charge and need to be present always.

Shouting or yelling from you will make any situation worse. Be prepared so that you can feel calm – remember you are the dominant one in this miniature herd.

Sorting Board - When you first make the introduction between the two pigs, have a sorting board ready just in case. If the pigs do begin to fight, you can put the sorting board between the pair to separate them.

You should never get yourself in between the fighting pigs as you will put yourself at risk of serious injury. Other alternatives to sorting boards include a trash can lid, or a piece of plywood board.

Separate Areas - After a short introduction, allow the pigs to have some space away from each other. Either in another enclosure outside or different rooms inside.

If the pigs are indoor pigs, consider installing a baby gate (make sure it's a sturdy design and you fit it securely).

Allow the pigs to see each other only briefly several times during the day. Keep close watch and remember that a pig could jump over the baby gate or knock it down.

Keep this going for about a week. You may choose to do this for longer depending on how the pigs respond to each other.

Once behaviors through the gate seem to be calmer, this may be the time to try and put the two pigs together for the first time.

If the Mini Pigs are to be kept outside, have a separate enclosure or pasture ready for them. In a similar way to the baby gate, have a piece of fence between them so that they can meet without having physical contact immediately.

Allow Plenty of Time - You may find that it takes a little while for the pigs to gradually get used to each other. Give the pigs as much time as they need; try not to hurry the process. Normally Mini Pigs would need at least a week of these short meetings through a gate or fence.

The First Scuffle – There will be inevitable fighting when the two pigs are allowed physical contact with each other. You will need to allow scuffling, but you will need to watch very closely – and have your sorting board at the ready. Even if one pig immediately retreats, this is extremely unlikely to be the end of it – stay and watch as there still may be fighting to come.

Once the fighting has subsided, the dominance will be established already. Clean off any wounds and treat cuts and abrasions. A vet will need to treat any wounds that are more serious.

This will be incredibly tense for you as the loving owner but this scuffle at the start should put an end to fighting – pigs have this natural need to work out their place in the hierarchy.

Chapter 8 – Becoming Piggy Prepared

Getting Ready

There are many items that you will need to have ready for your new pet Miniature Pig. This is because your Mini Pig is a unique pet that has individual needs.

Being prepared will help you be a good owner; realizing the needs of your Mini Pig and providing for them will make your pig feel happy and settle in with you and your family much more quickly.

You will find that there are few products that have been designed specifically for Mini Pigs.

This does not mean that they do not need items especially for them! Take your time and look around at different products.

Chapter 8 – Becoming Piggy Prepared

Check-List

Use the following as a check list so you know exactly what you need to buy and have prepared.

Sturdy Water and Food Bowl – Water and food bowls need to be substantial. In enthusiastic piggy fashion, your pig will eagerly and invariably try and tip the bowl over.

You can try and train your pig not to flip the bowl over but as well as this, it is preferable to find bowls that are more difficult to turn over due to their size and weight.

Look for a bowl that is heavy and larger. Even when piglets, Mini Pigs have very strong snouts and will easily turn a small bowl over. Use a bowl that they will grow into and try not to be tempted by the cute little bowls available at pet stores.

Pig Bed – Pigs do love to sleep, and they will find great comfort in a special place which is their pig bed. Find a bed that is soft and cozy. The bed will need to be large enough so that your Mini Pig can root into the bed.

The bed will need to be strong enough to support their weight – otherwise your Mini Pig will essentially be sleeping on the ground.

The bed will need to be low to the ground so that it is easy for the pig to climb in and out of. Also look for a bed that is easy to wash.

Pig Blankets – Pigs use blankets to root around in and they love them! They are essential items for your pig to stay warm and cuddle into.

It is probably beneficial to have several. You may want to keep them in different places around the house – and maybe put a couple into his / her bed.

Look for soft, large blankets that can be washed easily. The blankets will get dirty and some may get damaged.

It is not worth investing in expensive blankets, try looking for some that are on sale. When your pig is older, and you know each other much better, you may feel that you can trust your pig with a special blanket that may have cost you more money.

By Eirik Newth (This little pig went down to the river...) [CC BY 2.0 (http://creativecommons.org/licenses/by/2.0)], via Wikimedia Commons

Harness – Harnesses are available that have been specifically designed for Mini Pigs. A dog harness can also work. These seem to work the best for young piglets (even better than the harnesses designed for Mini Pigs).

Owners frequently report that it can be challenging to get the harness on and off their Mini Pigs.

It will be hugely beneficial to begin training your pig to wear a harness and walk on a leash at a young age – younger pigs tend to be more cooperative and willing to try new things. You may need to use treats for encouragement.

You will be able to use any kind of leash.

Litter Box and Puppy Pads – It may be that you encourage your Mini Pig to do toileting outside. However, it is usually advisable to provide a litter box and pet pads in the room where your pig will spend most of the day – and especially night. Note that a piglet will not have full bladder control until around 10 months old.

Some piggy owners use a ferret litter box. This is because it has a lower front side and so is easier for the Mini Pig to step into. Other owners find that a cat litter box works well – or as the pig gets larger, a storage box.

Puppy pads are great to put inside the litter box.

We explore other options in our section on '**Toilet Training**' in '**Chapter 13 – Everyday Care'.** Do not use cat litter as it is toxic for your pig – and he / she will undoubtedly have a go at eating it.

Food – It is easier if you are already stocked up on Mini Pig food (pellets) before you bring your new Micro Pig home. You will need to purchase food that is especially formulated for Mini Pigs.

Crate – A crate is a must-have and likely that you will need it to transport your Mini Pig home in the first place.

There are many kinds of crates available. You will need a large or extra-large dog crate. Some have flaps that open at the top (in addition to the main door where your pig will get in and out). This allows you to add items into the crate such as blankets or food and communicate with your pig and pet him / her without your pig being able to escape.

In addition to a means of transportation, a crate can also provide a safe space for your pig inside the house. This may be important, especially in the early days when you are introducing your pig to your home.

You may find the crate useful in terms of toilet training.

Additionally, the crate may be useful when you need to correct behavioral problems.

Ramps – It may be unfeasible to lift the full weight of your pig into your car.

This means you will need a ramp for your pig to access the car. Ensure that the angle of the ramp isn't too steep otherwise your Mini Pig will be unwilling to use it.

Consider whether you will need to install any ramps going into any of the doors of your home. A Mini Pig will be unable to manage many steps.

It is useful to begin ramp training when your Mini Pig is younger – this is usually when they are more willing to learn new things.

Further information on ramps can be found later on in **'Chapter 9 – Piggy Proofing your Home'** where there is a dedicated section on **'Ramps'**.

Playpen- This will allow your Mini Pig to be very near to the rest of the family but at the same time, your pig will be contained.

This may be useful to avoid accidents and to manage behavior while you are busy. There should be loads of room in the playpen for the Mini Pig to roam around in.

In the playpen, include a bed and some toys. He / she will be able to see out and still feel part of the family.

Make sure that the playpen is light so that you can move it into different rooms. It may also be useful when you are visiting family or friends.

Gates – Instead of (or in addition to) a playpen, you may prefer to use a baby gate. Use the gate to confine a pig to a safe space or even room. By having a baby gate instead of a closed door, your pig will still have the benefit of your company and will feel part of the family.

Sorting Board – These have been mentioned earlier in this book as an aid to introducing two pigs to one another.

In addition to this use, you may find that you need one with just the one pig. They can be useful in guiding a Mini Pig to a specific area that you need him / her to go. If you are dealing with an aggressive pig, then a sorting board can be used as a way of protecting yourself.

Cleaning Products – It is inevitable that your beloved Mini Pig will have several accidents when first settling down into your new home.

The best way to deal with this is simply being prepared – this is a temporary phase and it is easy to clean if you have cleaning materials readily available.

Ensure that you use cleaning products that eliminate all odors – this should stop your Mini Pig having an accident repeatedly in the same place.

Constructing a Pen

Mini Pigs really enjoy spending time outside, rooting, grazing, exploring and foraging around in the dirt. Even 'indoor house pigs' need plenty of time out in the yard.

The nature of foraging means that your yard will be turned upside down by a very strong and inquisitive snout.

To restrict 'destruction' to a certain part of your yard and to contain your pig, you will need to construct fencing to essentially make a piggy pen.

Consider how much space you can spare for your Mini Pig's enclosure. They do need plenty of room to root and to graze – at least 36 square meters (118 square foot) per pig.

Fencing needs to be strong and secure and completely escape proof. Your Mini Pig will enjoy checking out the strength of your fencing panels to the absolute limit.

Even the smallest of Mini Pigs are incredibly strong.

Chapter 8 – Becoming Piggy Prepared

To prevent your pig escaping, you will need to bury the fencing about 5 cm (2 inches) below the ground. All the rooting that your pig will do makes this necessary!

Don't rely on visitors coming in and closing the gate behind them – it will only take one person to forget to close the gate and your precious Mini Pig could find its way out.

The pen really does need to be properly secured and separated from the main yard.

By having that separation, you can check and guarantee that the Mini Pig's area is clear of debris – that snout will always be looking for things to eat whether good for him / her or not.

Chapter 8 – Becoming Piggy Prepared

Providing Protection

While outdoors, your Mini Pig will need some protection.

The outdoor space you provide needs to be able to protect your Mini Pig from predators. This could be any form of wildlife that may be a threat to your Micro Pig – consider what wildlife you may have in your local area – dogs, wolves, bears.

Additionally, your Mini Pig needs protecting from the harsh elements of the weather. An outdoor structure – house or enclosure.

In the warm summer months, your Mini Pig needs some shade so that it can escape the direct sunlight and heat of the day.

In the colder months, it will need protection from the cold, wind, rain or even snow.

It might be that you intend to keep your Mini Pig inside your house for the majority of time. It is just important to realize that your pig will very likely enjoy being outside – and that he / she will need some kind of protection while out there.

Pigs do not tolerate either extremes of temperature well. As well as grazing and foraging, they also like lying down to rest and they will prefer this in an enclosure that will give them a sense of safety and security.

You could purchase a large or extra-large dog house. Most important to consider is whether the house is large enough for your Mini Pig.

There are many ideas out there online showing how other owners have designed their own pet pig house. There are some fabulous designs that may inspire you to feel creative yourself.

Just ensure that your enclosure has 4 walls, a roof and an entrance door! It needs to keep your pig safe and also warm. Check that the roof is watertight so that it will definitely remain dry.

During the colder winter months, be sure to add in some insulation to keep your Micro Pig warm.

Straw and hay both provide excellent insulation. As well as keeping your pig warm, he / she will also enjoy eating the hay, so you will need to keep topping it up.

Provide enough hay or straw that they can bury themselves beneath it. It will soon get squashed down so you will then need to fluff it up and add more by the end of the week.

Be careful that the hay does not go moldy. If your Mini Pig eats moldy hay, they will end up with some health problems. So, do check regularly for moldy hay or straw, and obviously remove any that you find is moldy.

Blankets are also a popular option to add into the Mini Pig's house for an extra layer of warmth.

You could also cover windows and doors with blankets and rugs (including the entrance door). This will provide additional and much wanted extra warmth and insulation.

Chapter 9 – Piggy Proofing your Home

In addition to purchasing the 'check-list' items ready for your new pet pig, you will need to make some 'piggy proofing' adjustments to your home.

The aim of this is to make sure that your pig is safe and stays out of harms' way.

As well as keeping your new pet safe, you will also be taking precautions to keep damage to home and belongings at an absolute minimum.

Mini Pigs enjoy chewing on just about everything! Keep electrical cords out of the way, use child-proof locks for cupboards and even for your refrigerator.

Check that your furnishings are secure – pigs love to rub against / scratch themselves on everything (including walls and furniture).

This means that furniture that is not secured down could easily be knocked over. Even young piglets are much stronger than you would imagine.

Chapter 9 – Piggy Proofing your Home

Creating a Pig Safe Zone

As well as 'piggy proofing' your home, it will be invaluable if you have a space that is completely secure and safe for your pig. Somewhere that is free of hazards for your pig and where they can do no damage – this will mean that you can leave your Mini Pig alone knowing that all will be well.

This could be a very large play pen with toys, water and a litter box.

Or a dedicated room where you have no personal possessions that could be destroyed or damaged by your Mini Pig. Have everything set up and ready to be welcoming and comforting for your pig.

When you first bring your pet pig home, it may be that your new family member spends all of his / her time in this area. You can come into the room to bond with your pig and spend as much time as you can with him / her.

It will take the majority of Mini Pigs about 4 weeks to become accustomed to you, their new house and surroundings.

Chapter 9 – Piggy Proofing your Home

Install Locks and Utilize Gates

Mini Pigs are very curious animals and will be keen to explore the inside of your cupboards. You will need to protect your pig from poisonous items or even just food that he / she shouldn't eat – not to mention the fact that you probably don't want your cupboards rooted around in and turned upside down!

Child-proof locks will be a deterrent for your Mini Pig. But don't just rely on those – you will need to supervise and keep a careful watch. Make sure that your Mini Pig is not able to break through into the cupboard with his / her super strong snout.

Gates are a fabulous way of restricting your pig to certain areas of the house. By using a gate as opposed to a shut door, your pig will have the pleasure of your company (who may be in the next room) plus will feel more like a valued member of the herd.

It also enables you to have some space where you don't need to worry about either the safety of your pig or of your possessions.

Chapter 9 – Piggy Proofing your Home

Ramps

Consider the stairs in your home. There may be steps leading to a front or back door – or the main stairs inside the house.

Some Mini Pigs can manage the stairs, especially when they are younger. However, in the wild pigs do not climb or jump. Stairs can put the health and safety of your Micro Pig at risk.

The majority of Mini Pigs will be scared of going up and down the stairs and it is potentially dangerous for them.

If a Mini Pig does fall down the steps, a risk of bone fracture is incredibly high. As the Mini Pig gets older, it is likely that they will struggle with the stairs and be very vulnerable to falling. Pigs who are overweight will not be able to use the stairs at all.

Ramps are an alternative to stairs and pigs find ramps much easier to manage.

It is inadvisable to allow Mini Pigs to go up and down more than a couple of steps. If the steps lead to an area where you would like your pig to go, then a ramp may be the best way forward.

It may sensible to avoid your pig going to the upstairs part of your home. The stairs are potentially hazardous, and you may not want a ramp going up the main stairs of your home.

The slope of the ramp must be gentle – a Mini Pig will be very reluctant to use a ramp that is steep. You may need to extend the overall length of the ramp so that it ends up being longer than the steps.

Be sure that the ramp is not a slippery material – you may consider adding carpet, sandpaper or other tacky material to give your Mini Pig more grip.

The ramp obviously needs to be extremely sturdy to withstand the weight of the Mini Pig. A pig will be frightened to use a ramp that moves (even if ever so slightly) under their weight.

You will need to take the time to train your Micro Pig to use the ramp. If your Mini Pig stops using the ramp for an extended period, it is likely that you will need to do more training again.

Chapter 9 – Piggy Proofing your Home

Organizing your Home

Just like when you have a baby or toddler in the house, the way you arrange your home and belongings will need some adjustment. When you invite your Mini Pig to live in your home with you, you will need to consider the following points.

Garbage Cans out of the way – Your Mini Pig would love to create an enormous mess and have a rummage through your rubbish. To protect your Mini Pig from the hazards that may be lurking inside your garbage and to prevent unnecessary mess, ensure that all garbage cans are in an area where your Mini Pig cannot go.

Food out of the way – Put all food out of reach of your pet pig. This may be up high, so they are unable to reach it. Even more preferable would be behind a closed and locked door.

Pigs tend to forget about any rules and training when they get a whiff of food – except where you are using food to train them of course.

Ensure floor is clear – Mini Pigs are like vacuum cleaners – if they find something on the floor, they will definitely eat it. Like when you have a baby in the house, make sure that the floor is clear. Look out for items such as rubber bands, erasers, balloons, latex gloves, small toys. All of these types of things can be swallowed and could potentially get stuck inside the throat.

Valuables out of the way – When you invite your pig to play and explore in your home, ensure that all valuable possessions are well out of the way. A pig seems to have a way of managing to break things with tremendous ease!

Chapter 10 – Enriching the Life of your Mini Pig

The Value of Enrichment

Animal enrichment is the process of a providing a stimulating environment for your pet. Enrichment involves improving the environment to provide an outlet for natural behaviors and needs through physical and mental challenges.

To decide how you could enrich your home to make it a more interesting and welcoming place to live, it is important to consider how pigs live in the wild. This gives an indication of the environmental needs of the Mini Pig.

Pigs that are feral spend vast amounts of time foraging for food. The remaining time tends to be spent resting. Pigs make use of their incredible sense of smell to find sources of food. They use their strong snout to dig into the earth, looking for invertebrates, fungi, roots and seeds.

While thinking of ways to enrich the life of your mini pig, you are essentially providing your pig with an environment that imitates their natural way of life – they can behave in a similar way to how they would if they were feral.

This natural behavior will make your pig feel happy and will guarantee a fulfilled life. Indeed, a pig that is busy will be a happy pig.

An environment that includes no companionship or stimulation will result in a Mini Pig who is agitated, destructive and likely aggressive.

There are various aspects to enrichment including physical exercise, mental exercise, training and interactions with you and your family, scents, sounds, food related, new objects, new environments and simply making the most of the home environment.

Enrichment activities will be interesting, stimulating and varied. With a variety of activities, you will be enriching the life of your Mini Pig on an everyday basis.

Chapter 10 – Enriching the Life of your Mini Pig

Rooting Boxes

You can make your Mini Pig his / her very own rooting box (or probably boxes) inside your home. This satisfies a pig's instinctive desire to root and forage for food.

If a pig spends much of his / her time indoors then a rooting box will be a really important part of your pig's life. Just like pigs in the wild, with a rooting box, your pig can make good use of their snout and have a much loved and satisfying rummage around for food. The very favorite pastime of pigs!

The rooting box can be made from any container that has sides that are low enough for the pig to step into and big enough that the pig can turn around once inside it.

You might use a large plastic container, a wooden box, a small kiddie swimming pool or a large dog cage.

Try filling the bottom with smooth flat stones or rocks, plastic balls, blankets, an assortment of toys or loosely crumpled newspaper.

To imitate foraging, sprinkle a portion of the pig's food into the rooting box. You could sprinkle things such as pig pellets, coconut oil or cheerios. Your Mini Pig will love exploring and foraging for treats. It may even be so popular with your Mini Pig that you decide to sprinkle entire meals into the rooting box.

To retain interest for your pig, it may be beneficial to change the contents of the rooting box from time to time. This way, they will have a different rooting experience.

It is worth remembering that it is important not to overfeed your Mini Pig. Consequently, any treats or food provided for your Micro Pig in the rooting box should be included when you calculate how many calories you are giving.

Sand and Hay Boxes

Like the Rooting Boxes, sand and hay boxes can be made from anything – a wooden box, plastic container or small kiddy pool.

Some owners find that it is best to put the rooting objects into a dog crate. This makes for a less messy activity as everything will be a little more contained.

Sand Box - Your Mini Pig will adore rooting and foraging around in soft sand. Sandboxes are another excellent enrichment activity for Mini Pigs. Try hiding small treats like popcorn or cheerios in the sand.

Your pig will use his / her incredible sense of smell to find the treats, also satisfying their instinct to root and forage.

This activity will require your supervision as you will need to ensure that your pig doesn't decide to eat the sand too!

Hay Box – Hay is the perfect thing for rooting and foraging around in. It is soft and as they root into it; the treats will move around making for a greater challenge. You could use any snack inside the Hay Box.

Toys

The popular toys with Mini Pigs are always the ones related to food. Suitable toys include treat balls, treat dispensers and food balls.

Treat Balls - These come in a variety of shapes and sizes. Some are quite easy, and some can be challenging for your Mini Pig.

The treat ball basically works in that the pig will use his / her natural rooting behavior and will eventually be rewarded with a snack. Some treat balls are made specifically for Mini Pigs but some that have been made for dogs, cats and horses, can also be suitable.

A wide assortment of snacks can be used inside the treat ball – normal feed pellets, any assortment of unsalted nuts or seeds, black oil sunflower seeds, cranberries, oatmeal, natural whole grains, raisins, cheerios, puffed rice cereal, or healthy low sugar whole grain cereals (Shredded Wheat, Bran Flakes).

Treat balls are a very satisfying activity for Mini Pigs.

Treat Dispensers – These you will be able to make yourself at home. Simply find a bottle or food container (small water bottle, big two-liter bottles, used oatmeal canister, yogurt pot, margarine tub) –any container that is safe.

Either leave the lid open or drill / punch holes into the bottle. Make the holes of varying sizes – bigger holes will mean that you can choose from a wider range of snacks to go inside but on the flip side, the food will come out more quickly and will be less of a challenge for your Mini Pig.

The fewer holes you make will prove more of a challenge for your pig, therefore providing more stimulation and exercise.

Food Balls – An open ball (with holes) works as another great toy for Mini Pigs. Stuff lettuce, vegetables, grass into an open ball so that your pig will have to work hard to pull the food out. Rubber webbed balls designed for dog's work very well. Whiffle balls also make an excellent choice.

Think about covering up some of the holes with tape to make for a greater challenge.

As a variation, you could stuff the ball with scrunched up newspaper or pieces of fabric - with pellets or treats wrapped up inside. This will certainly keep your pig busy for quite some time!

Like the rooting box, you will need to make sure you include any food given in this way as part of your daily diet plan for your pet pig.

For an additional variation to the treat balls and dispensers, try hanging them for a low ceiling or the top of a crate. This will provide your pet pig with extra physical exercise and will take them a little longer, making the enrichment activity more involved and stimulating.

Try putting a hole through a plastic water ball and hanging it up with a few treats at the bottom. Your Mini Pig will have to nudge the bottle to make it tip and flip over so that the treats fall out. You could hang large pieces of fruit and vegetables up just high enough that your pig has to work hard to reach it.

Balls and Buckets – Some Mini Pigs will enjoy pushing a ball (large ball such as a soccer ball) or a bucket around the yard. You could also try toys designed for dogs, horses and even toddlers. Mini Pigs seem to prefer toys that can roll around as they can nudge them around with their snout.

Blankets

Pigs really do adore blankets. You will find that your Mini Pig carries them around to different rooms. They love to root in the blankets, and curl up underneath them and sleep.

Pigs living in the wild tend to all sleep together – essentially in a pile! This indicates that pigs prefer to be warm and cozy and it is likely that the blanket gives them a sense of that warmth they instinctively need and desire. When a pig roots into the blanket, he / she is imitating foraging again – exploring with the snout.

Scratch Pads

Scratching is very natural behavior for a Mini Pig. Indeed, they will use anything they can to scratch themselves against – including walls and furniture. Consider putting some scratch pads up around the house. These will provide your Piggy with a very satisfying place to scratch and will hopefully encourage him / her to leave other walls alone.

You can purchase scratch pads specifically designed for animals. Alternatively, you could use a rigid brush and attach it to the side of a building, wall or fence. The brush idea works particularly well in outdoor areas.

A good scratch is very satisfying for a pig!

Be very aware of furniture that is not secured to the wall. The strength of a Mini Pig scratching him or herself against it could be enough to knock it over. You may need to secure furniture to the walls as an additional safety measure.

Chapter 10 – Enriching the Life of your Mini Pig

Glorious Mud

We all know that pigs love to roll in mud. This is to help them keep cool and is important for both large farm pigs and pet Mini Pigs. Because of their high sensitivity to heat (and no sweat glands), cooling down by rolling in the mud is necessary to prevent heat related stress and health problems.

Coating their skin in mud protects the Mini Pig from the sun and also from insects.

You will find that your Mini Pig will dig its' own holes in the yard to create a cool spot to lay down in on hot and sunny days.

Enhance your pig's experience by creating their very own extremely muddy mud hole! Use the hose to drench loads of water into a low area / ditch. This may be a naturally occurring area or you may find you need to dig an area out. Your Mini Pig will delight in rolling and wallowing in all that mud!

Chapter 10 – Enriching the Life of your Mini Pig

Pools

When it is hot, your Mini Pig will love a kiddie pool. It's the perfect place for a pig to cool down.

Plus, it is a fantastic enrichment activity.

You can use an inflatable pool or a rigid plastic pool. If your pig seems to find the pool slippery or seems a little nervous, try adding a rubber bathmat with suction cups for additional grip.

An extra pleasure for your pig is a floating meal in the pool! Many vegetables will float in the pool – the snack is no longer simply something to eat but a stimulating activity, something mentally and physically challenging for your pet pig.

Some confident pigs that are really fond of the water will even enjoy searching for treats that sink to the bottom of the pool. They will snorkel right down to the bottom of the pool in search of their treat.

Chapter 10 – Enriching the Life of your Mini Pig

Obstacle Courses

Obstacle Courses are a wonderful enrichment activity for your pet Mini Pig. Additionally, they build on training skills, physical skills and behaviors. Very stimulating, they provide a challenge both mentally and physically. Plus, they are a really fun way for you to bond together. Be sure to try it otherwise you and your pig will be missing out!

Pigs tend to enjoy going through a tunnel as part of an obstacle course. They might need a little encouragement at first. Put some treats at the entrance to the tunnel and some more half-way in the tunnel and some on the exit side. Be sure to move around to the exit side of the tunnel yourself and be ready with lots of praise.

Practice this a few times and once familiar, it will be a favorite activity for your Mini Pig. When walking through the tunnel, use a cue word such as 'tunnel'. Say this every time piggy is in the tunnel so that they will connect the word to the activity.

Once you observe that your pig is enjoying the experience, you will no longer need to provide treats as an incentive.

You will simply be able to use the cue word – 'tunnel' and piggy will go right on in.

Your obstacle course will improve your pig's agility and will help keep fitness levels up.

Include obstacles that piggy can walk in and around (guide with your hand so that your pig knows where you want them to go). Have your pig walk up and down a ramp or step over something; use large cardboard boxes, balls and hoops.

Think about including plastic crates – maybe put them at the end with something to eat tucked up inside. Your pig will have fun and have a challenge trying to figure out how to reach the treat.

You can vary the obstacle course – make it as simple or long or short as you fancy. Vary it and pretty soon you will feel confident setting up a course that you know your piggy will love.

Chapter 11 – Introducing the Micro Pig to your Herd

Mixing Micro Pigs with Children

Guaranteed that your child will love the idea of a pet pig! How cool, unusual and unquestionably cute. However, there are some important considerations to make.

Pigs are herd animals and need to find their place in the herd. They will try and establish dominance over 'members of the herd' that they see as weak.

Pigs seem to recognize children as smaller and therefore will sometimes try and establish their dominance over them.

Pigs will occasionally try to dominate over an adult member of the household; although your pig will soon stop providing behavior is managed correctly.

However, this behavior can be much more challenging to address where children are involved.

Older children may be able to establish dominance effectively with the pig, but you will need to invest a lot of energy and time with a younger child interacting with the pig.

It is not true to say that pigs do not get on with children - simply to point out that the pigs need to establish a pecking order within the herd and this can make it difficult where children live in the household.

This next point is clearly an obvious one, but worth a quick mention. As with other pets, you will need to teach your child to be always gentle with your pet pig. Explain that even when your child thinks that the pig has been naughty, he / she must never hit or be rough with your pig.

Intelligent as we all know pigs are, a pig will remember if they have been hit, even if only once.

Mixing Micro Pigs with other Pets

Pigs are social animals and thrive on the company of other animals. Indeed, other pets will be an important part of your pig's life.

Ideally a pig would like another piggy friend – this is not always possible or practical. Indeed, a fully grown mini pig will take up a lot of space due to its' size – also a pet pig requires a lot of energy and commitment.

Some owners prefer to use other pets as companions for their pig; these may be already part of the household or you may consider adding them as a companion for your already established pig.

It is generally safe to introduce your piggy to other pets that are not predators. This may include guinea pigs, rabbits, lizards, ponies to name just a few. Always be there to supervise and make sure that both animals are safe and not feeling stressed in any way.

Chapter 11 – Introducing the Micro Pig to your Herd

Mixing Micro Pigs with Cats

Pigs and cats can make superb companions and it seems that they tend to get on very well together.

Pigs are sociable animals and if you are considering a companion for your pig but feel that you cannot manage another pig, a cat may well be the answer.

Chapter 11 – Introducing the Micro Pig to your Herd

First Introductions with your Micro Pig and Cat

Make a slow and gradual introduction and watch out for body language of both pig and cat. You need to be absolutely certain about their interactions before leaving them alone together.

Pigs are naturally very curious animals and tend to sniff anything that is new to them. This will probably include your cat and be aware that this may be a frightening experience for your cat.

For the first introduction between your Micro Pig and Cat, it may be worth keeping the pig in a small enclosure; this will allow the cat to get used to it.

A baby gate can also be very useful for a first introduction. In either case, both animals will be able to observe each other without direct physical contact. This should foster a sense of safety and diminish threatening behaviors.

Otherwise consider introducing them to each other in an outside space where territory is viewed as neutral. It is likely that your cat will initially leap away and hide. But this is not necessarily disastrous as it will allow the cat to explore its new companion at its own pace.

Feeding your Micro Pig and Cat

Establishing a way to feed both Micro Pig and Cat will require some planning and forethought. Separate feeding times and areas for your Micro Pig and Cat will probably be essential.

The pig will be so fond of its' food that it will try and eat all food near and available to it – this will include your cats' dinner.

As cats normally like to graze and have food and water available to them all day, you will need to find a special place where your cat can come to eat without being bothered by your Micro Pig. Not impossible - but do think about where could be your cat's special place; that could also be blocked off to your pig.

Micro Pigs and Cats – Companions?

Cats and micro pigs can make fantastic companions, but it is obviously not guaranteed. It will depend on the nature and temperament of both cat and micro pig. It may be that they interact together, or it may be that they live side by side tolerating each other.

They will work together to establish a pecking order; it may be that the cat is dominant over the pig – or that the pig is dominant over the cat. Personality dependent, only time will tell. Whilst no guarantees can be given, this certainly adds another interesting element to the herd!

Mixing Micro Pigs with Dogs

Dogs and micro pigs can be excellent playmates and provide much wanted companionship for one another. However, they do not always get along, it really depends on the personalities of the micro pig and the dog.

In the natural world, dogs are predators and micro pigs are prey. It is therefore imperative that you watch over all interactions to ensure the safety of your micro pig.

To complicate interactions further, pigs do tend to be very stubborn. This means that they are very reluctant to back down if they come into a disagreement with a dog; this can result in some dangerous situations.

The micro pig will not be able to defend itself against a dog, so the micro pig will always come off worse.

It may be that interaction between the micro pig and dog begins as friendly play - but 'friendly play' can become rough quite abruptly. If things are allowed to get out of hand, the pig will always be the loser; and tragically the outcome can be disastrous for the pig.

Before considering keeping a pig and a dog together, have an honest reflection on the personality of your dog – are they tolerant of other animals, gentle and under your control? If yes, then the relationship between Micro Pig and Dog can work.

First Introductions with your Micro Pig and Dog

When introducing your micro pig to your dog for the first time, make sure that it is a gentle, brief and calm moment.

Consider using a baby gate for their very first interaction. This way they can see each other but still have their own personal space and safe zone.

You will then have an idea about how they will react to each other before they have direct physical contact. This will also mean that you have full control over the introduction and will be able to manage any eventuality.

An alternative option is for your dog and micro pig to meet each other for the first time outside. This may help as outside is seen by both as neutral territory.

This should not be a stressful encounter for anybody and you should not consider it as such. By organizing the 'introduction' you are simply ensuring a manageable situation that will be beneficial to yourself, your dog and your micro pig.

The first introduction is very often uneventful in that neither animal displays much interest in the other. Consider this a solid foundation for plenty of interaction and socializing to come in the future.

Feeding your Micro Pig and Dog

As your micro pig will be inevitably quite obsessed by food it may be beneficial to organize separate mealtimes for your dog and micro pig. This will avoid your micro pig trying to demolish the food you have just left out for your dog (as well as its' own food).

Perhaps consider feeding your micro pig first and then keeping him / her separate (inside a crate, different room – whatever works for you) while your dog eats.

Chapter 11 – Introducing the Micro Pig to your Herd

Micro Pigs and Dogs – Companions?

We have shown how it is very possible to keep pigs and dogs in the same household (or herd!).

Just be aware that you will need to watch over all interactions between the micro pig and the dog.

More than likely, they will both benefit and enjoy their interactions with each other over time. When you need to leave them, simply keep them separated. Just consider your dog's natural temperament and whether he / she is tolerant of other animals. And always remain vigilant.

Chapter 12 – Understanding Behavior and Training

The First Days and what to Expect

You will be feeling very excited but most likely a little nervous when you bring your new pet pig home for the first time. But this is probably nothing compared to how your Mini Pig will be feeling.

He / she is likely to feel scared and confused during the first few days. Nothing about you or their new home will be familiar to them. Every scent will be brand new.

Normal behavior for a Mini Pig in the first few days will be running away, trying to hide, lots of squealing and grinding teeth. Be prepared to be very patient! They are prey animals in the wild and this means that they will constantly be on the alert to danger – they will instinctively want to flee from new sounds, movements and touch.

Even if your piglet has been well socialized with the breeder, they will still be scared and timid in their new surroundings for the first few days or weeks in their new home.

After all, your piglet has just left their litter mates, parents and caretakers for their first few months of life – this is all they have ever known.

All they will want from you is a quiet cozy space that makes them feel safe. This will help your pig settle more quickly. They will need plenty of time before they can feel truly comfortable in their new home with you.

If you plan to designate a particular room to your pig, allow him / her to adjust to only this room at first.

Otherwise think about using a laundry room or utility room for your pig in these first few days.

They will not appreciate roaming around and exploring their new house yet.

If you are not able to devote a room to your pig, try and provide them with an enclosed area. Maybe use a playpen or large crate – or install a baby gate to create an enclosed space.

The important thing is that they have a small space that they can feel is their own private space – somewhere small, cozy and quiet.

Pigs enjoy being warm and obviously being fed – frequently! Ensure that they have access to their water bowl at all times (make sure the water bowl is heavy to limit the number of times it will be tipped over).

Being warm is very important for a Mini Pig and will help them to feel comfortable and relaxed. If you are bringing home a piglet under 5 weeks old, consider utilizing a heat lamp. If you have a piglet over 5 weeks, a Heat Pad designed for pets will be very gratifying.

Provide soft blankets. Mini Pigs love to burrow inside them and this natural behavior will help them to feel secure. Your pig will also enjoy snuggling into their bed.

On the opposite side to their bed, provide a litter box. Pigs are extremely clean animals and will want their litter box as far away from their bed as possible.

If your Mini Pig was transported in a crate, leave the crate open near your pig. This will regarded as a place of safety – somewhere to hide when they are feeling overwhelmed by their new environment.

Let them settle into a small space while they gradually get to know you and their new surroundings.

It is very tempting to try and rush through this settling in process, but it is necessary for your pig. Be patient, your new pet pig will have plenty of time to explore their new home – and the people living in it!

Bonding with your Pet Pig

Bonding is about building up a relationship of love and trust between owner and Mini Pig.

Pigs are not naturally social and trusting. They are instinctively nervous and distrusting since they are prey animals in the wild.

This means that bonding with your pig is a process – it may be a long process, but it will be highly rewarding and thoroughly worthwhile.

For your pig to become a 'true pet', you will need to work hard to bond with your pig and essentially to socialize him / her. Once trust is established, you will find that your pet pig is extraordinarily affectionate and very very sociable!

Allow your Mini Pig plenty of time and space to adjust to his / her new home environment and new family. Pigs will appreciate some personal space and the most important thing for them is that they feel safe.

Very importantly, avoid sudden movements and make any movements towards your pig very slow and gentle. Keep noise to a minimum and be very calm around your new pig.

It will be immensely useful if you can learn how the breeder or carers at the sanctuary interacted with your Mini Pig. Find out how they held the piglets, trained them, rewarded them and bonded with them. By keeping some of these techniques the same, the bonding and socialization process with your Mini Pig should be easier and swifter.

In the first few days, provide your Mini Pig with lots of opportunities to get to know you – and trust you.

Sit on the floor near your pig but don't give them any attention at first. Just make sure you are on the same level as you will look much less threatening. Sit down or even lay on the ground. Take your phone with you – or a book and be patient!

Allow them to get familiar with your scent and know that you will cause them no harm. Remain calm and quiet –

don't approach your pig but instead wait for him / her to come to you.

You will gradually build up a bond with your Mini Pig. Simply by sitting near your pig while they eat, rest and sleep. Soon enough, they will come up to you and climb on you!

Try to wait for your first cuddle until your pig shows you that they are ready. They will eventually climb onto your lap and this will be your opportunity for that incredibly special first cuddle.

Your Mini Pig will need to feel confident and trust you before they will enjoy being held and cuddled. When your piglet is ready to be held, ensure that you support their back and front legs – and neck / head.

You may try to hold your piglet and find that they are not confident enough yet. They will let you know by squealing, biting and trying to escape from your arms. Don't worry, it will come. It simply means you need to wait a little longer for your pig to feel confident in their new home.

Remember to talk and grunt to your Mini Pig. They will soon start to communicate with you and respond to your grunts. Over time, you will learn what the sound of your Mini Pig's sounds, tones and grunts meant. Pigs really respond positively to communication and it forms an important part of the bond between you both.

This floor time will gradually create trust and your pig will begin to feel confident coming near you, knowing that you will not try to pick them up.

As you sit on the floor, try using pig pellets or treats to gain their trust. First place some a short distance away from you. Your Mini Pig is very likely to come and enjoy the treat. You can then place the next treat even nearer you and continue this exercise until they are coming right up to you.

Eventually, your Mini Pig will be accepting of your touching them as they come near you.

Note that pigs will be scared if you try and reach over their head and touch them like you would a dog. More acceptable to them is if you reach out your open hand under their chin. Keep this movement as slow as possible.

Another opportunity to bond with your new pet pig is unexpectedly when they are asleep.

When they are napping, very gently touch your pig. You will often find that a pig who has his tummy rubbed while sleeping will roll over for more! The more the pig is petted in this way, the more secure the bond will be between owner and pig.

After a few weeks, you will be able to hold your piglet on your lap or chest while you are watching television. They will be comfortable falling asleep on you. Your smell, heartbeat and breathing will all become very familiar and comforting to them.

The more floor time, touching, holding and just being nearby, the quicker your pet pig will bond with you and build up that special relationship of trust.

The Value of Training

Training your Mini Pig will build on the bonds you have established together. The importance of training is paramount to having a pet pig that is easy going and a good housemate.

Training establishes and continually reinforces you as the leader of the herd. It encourages good behavior; enables your pig to cooperate and follow your instructions; and minimizes the chances of aggressive behavior.

As soon as the bonding process has begun, and your Mini Pig has started to familiarize him / her self with you, you are ready to begin teaching tricks and basic skills. Your pig will follow your commands.

In this way, you are teaching your pig ways to stay safe and out of danger. Additionally, and very importantly, they are learning to cooperate so that you can enjoy enrichment and health based activities together.

Very significantly, training establishes you, the owner, as dominant over your pig.

This is completely necessary; your Mini Pig needs to know that you are in charge always. A pig who thinks he / she is head of the herd will be aggressive and uncooperative. This would obviously not make for a good pet.

The process of training your Mini Pig is highly rewarding and will be very satisfying to you as the owner. You can teach your pig to do virtually anything – this is thanks to the food you give as a reward!

Pigs respond incredibly well to food as a motivation for their training. Offer food as a reward when your Mini Pig follows commands, learns new tricks and skills. Give something that is small and quick to eat (examples include pig pellets, cheerios, shredded wheat, pieces of apple or halved grapes).

Make sure that you use healthy treats as rewards – remember that even what you give as a treat incentive counts towards your pig's daily intake of calories.

Additionally, realize that you can give a very small treat – your pig will perform the trick equally as enthusiastically whether you offer one cheerio or a whole handful.

Restrict training sessions to short periods of time. This ensures that your pig is focused on training and doesn't begin to lose concentration and feel distracted.

If you notice that your pig seems to be losing focus, simply quit for the time being and try again later or the following day.

If you are the owner of two Mini Pigs, it will probably be easier to limit training to one pig at a time. The two pigs together can be a distraction for each other and there will be inevitable competition over the food you are offering as rewards for good behavior.

As we discuss in the following Chapter, pigs thrive on routine. Make sure that training is part of your pig's daily routine. Choose a time where your pig seems alert and focused.

Avoid times where your pig is ready for a meal and may be too hungry to concentrate. Your pig may enjoy a better nights' sleep if they practice a little training before bedtime.

Training should be a very enjoyable experience for both you and your Mini Pig. It will build upon the trust you have built up together. It is an enriching experience for your pig, providing mental and physical challenges that will be stimulating.

He / she will come to love the attention you give, praise, communication - and also any treats offered! It will reinforce the bond between you and make it even stronger. It will also ensure that your pet pig is well behaved and will reduce destructive behavior massively.

Clicker Training

Clicker training is a fantastic way to train your Mini Pig. Behavior that is good is marked by using a clicker. This tells your pig exactly when they are doing the right thing. It is a very positive way of training and Mini Pigs tend to respond well to it.

The crucial difference between clicker training and food incentive training is that the clicker allows you to tell your pig exactly which behavior earned it the reward. This information is given by a distinct and unique sound; a click, which occurs at the same time as the anticipated behavior.

Clicker training complements food incentive training. The idea is that the pig hears the click at exactly the same time as he / she performs the trick (for example sits down). Almost immediately after that, you will present your pig with the treat.

By hearing the click at a precise time, your pig will know exactly which behavior you are rewarding.

Without using the clicker technique, your pig may not connect the reward with that action. They may even associate it with another action that was completely unintended and maybe not even noticed by you.

With the click, a trainer can exactly 'mark' behavior so that the pig recognizes precisely which behavior earned the reward. Once you have clicked at the precise time the pig performs an action, you can then present your pig with a treat to eat. Even a very quick and subtle behavior can be clicked.

A click is a unique sound for your pig; it always means that because of that particular action, they will now receive a treat. This is unlike your voice which varies in emotion and meaning. The click is exactly the same every time it is heard - and it means exactly the same thing – treat is coming!

Clickers are very inexpensive. They are easily available online as well as in pet stores.

Alternatively, you can simply make a similar sound with your mouth. Just ensure that you only use this noise when you are clicker training and at no other times.

Once your pig has learnt a particular behavior, you will not need to use the clicker (or food incentives). Try maintaining behavior by giving treats occasionally and simply giving lots of praise.

Learned cues and behaviors often have their own real-life rewards. For example, you may request that your pigs sit down before you present him / her with dinner – or you may ask your pig to 'come' so you can show him / her something that you know will be of interest like a new toy or rooting box.

Useful Commands

Come to Name – Arguably the most important skill to teach your Mini Pig is to 'come' on command. You may decide to simply use your pig's name or ask them to 'come'.

This is an incredibly useful command that will help your pig to cooperate with day to day tasks and routines.

Your Mini Pig will be able to recognize its' name from a very young age – but this is very different to getting your pig to come to you when you call their name.

Begin by saying the word 'come' every time you give your pig a meal (or if you prefer also use your pig's name). Use this phrase every single time you offer a treat or give any food for 2 – 3 days. Then try calling your pig from increased distances.

Always reward with praise and / or a healthy treat. Over the next few days, offer less treats and eventually simply give lots of praise and the treat will become unnecessary.

No – Another extremely useful command and one that you will undoubtedly need to use on occasion.

Pigs tend to learn short commands such as 'no' very easily and quickly. For this reason, try to say 'no' to your pig only when it is necessary to do so. For example, when your pig is behaving in an unacceptable way.

Say 'no' in a firm and reasonably loud voice (definitely no shouting though). Also, you may want to raise your hand to show stop – or point a finger to show that you are not pleased with that behavior. After a while, you will be able to simply raise your hand to demonstrate stop – or point your finger.

Try to use the command 'no' as little as possible. Instead focus on positive reinforcement. Praise good behavior and say a phrase such as 'good pig'.

Using Command Words – Many useful skills and behaviors are taught through word repetition and consistency. For example, using the word 'bed' every time your pig is put into bed will mean that over time, if you say the word 'bed', piggy will go to bed independently - without you needing to put them into bed yourself.

Over time you will think of command words that will be useful in the routine you have with your pig. Other frequently used command words are 'toilet' or 'harness'.

Sit – This command is slightly more difficult to teach and consequently, you will need to be more patient! However, it is a good skill to teach and will prove useful. You may want your pig to sit while waiting for something to happen (such as dinner!).

Your Mini Pig will probably already be familiar with the idea of a treat as a reward from earlier training.

While teaching your pig to sit, first show your pig the treat. Put it in front of the snout and then lift it slowly up and over the head – they will follow the treat with their snout. Say 'sit' and continue to raise the treat (with the snout still following treat). Eventually the pigs bottom will touch the floor and they will be sitting! As soon as the bottom touches the floor, offer the pig the treat and give lots of praise; also repeating 'sit'.

This trick will take longer to accomplish – but your pig will be able to sit on command with a little practice.

Back – Another very useful command. Your pig will inevitably explore areas where they should not go and will start rooting into something you don't want them to. The 'back' command is designed to make them stop.

When your pig roams into an area where they should not go, step towards the pig saying 'back' with each step. Be sure to be quick with praise when your pig starts to move back. Begin with just a couple of steps away from your pig and later increase the distance.

Once your Mini Pig has established this command, he / she will move back when you say the word 'back' and you will not need to move towards your pig yourself.

As with all other commands, on occasion you may need to use your body language in addition to the words, especially if your Mini Pig is very reluctant to move back!

Stay – This can be more difficult for the pig to master as their instinct will be not to stay but go in search of their treat / reward. The secret to success is to keep the treat out of piggy's sight.

First get your pig to sit and then repeat 'stay'. It is helpful to also use a hand gesture or finger point (whichever you use for 'no'). Once your pig has managed to sit still for a brief moment, give the treat and offer lots of praise. Over time, start to wait longer and encourage your pig to 'stay' before you offer the treat.

Gradually, you will be able to say 'stay' and then take several steps back; repeat 'stay' and pause for a few moments before returning to your pig with their reward. And of course, offer lots and lots of praise.

Be patient and over time, your pig will obediently learn to stay on your command.

Dance – This trick basically gets your pig to turn in circles – the reward is given when your pig turns to the left or right. This is easy to teach and extremely effective, and lots of fun too!

Teach this trick by holding up a treat over the top of your pig. Move the treat in a large circle, this will encourage your pig to use his feet to turn.

Some owners may prefer to use the phrase 'spin' and others may simply say 'left' and 'right'. Either way, your pig will enjoy performing a little dance, especially for a treat!

Shake Hands – To begin teaching this trick, start by very softly touching the back of piggy's hoof and say 'shake' – then offer a reward snack.

Once this part of the trick has become established, you will be able to put more pressure against the back of the hoof without causing upset. Some pigs will tolerate this very happily and others will take longer to adjust.

Over time, you will actually be able to lift their hoof; say 'shake' and then give the treat. Gradually start to sometimes offer a treat and other times just plenty of praise.

You can either offer your foot to shake or crouch down and stretch your hand out.

Soon enough when you say 'shake', your pig will put out his hoof and touch your hand or foot.

Wave – Once you have established shaking hands as a trick, you are ready to teach your Mini Pig to wave.

Simply say 'shake' but stand back a little and do not stretch out hand or foot. In the absence of your hand or foot, your pig will wave her hoof.

Once you have started doing this a few times, start saying 'wave' as he / she waves her hoof.

Harness and Leash Training

You will appreciate harness and leash training if you start this as soon as you can with your piglet (or older pig as soon as they arrive in your home).

When pigs are younger, they tend to be more willing to try new things. There will come a time where you need to take your pig out on a leash and your pig will be mighty reluctant unless this is something you have practiced.

Remember that as your baby piglet grows larger and heavier, it will not always be possible for you to carry him / her. It is essential training as you will need to take your Mini Pig to the vet – they may travel in the crate to the vet but you will need your pig on the harness and leash to get into the Veterinary Clinic.

What's more, taking your pig out is fun. You can visit the pet store together and there may be special events that you would enjoy taking your pig to. And you and your pig will enjoy exploring your neighborhood together.

You can purchase harnesses that are specially designed for Mini Pigs. Some owners find that harnesses designed for dogs also work well (this is especially true for piglets).

Collars are unsuitable for Mini Pigs. As pigs have very thick necks, a collar would not be comfortable for your pig and may cause a risk of choking.

Practice putting on the harness almost as soon as you bring your new pet pig home. Make practice sessions short so that your pig does not experience stress.

Micro Pigs are usually very reluctant to have a harness put on and are likely to protest. You will need to stay very calm and be patient.

Use simple command words such as 'harness on' and 'harness off' while you are training so that your pig knows what is happening – this will help in the future so that they know what you are doing.

Once you have the harness in position, distract your piggy friend with a little treat to eat. They will hopefully be enjoying something to eat while you can secure the harness and make any necessary adjustments.

When the harness is secure, leave it on for a couple of hours or so while you let your pig relax and play. This will allow your pig to adjust to the harness and realize that it will cause him / her no harm. She may protest initially but will become accustomed relatively quickly.

Repeat taking the harness on and off several times before you try using the leash as well. Wait until your pig seems comfortable and relaxed wearing the harness.

Chapter 12 – Understanding Behavior and Training

In the beginning, lay down a trail of treats that mark out where you want piggy to walk. This will help illustrate what you want your pig to do - and assists tremendously in their understanding and cooperation.

After your pig comprehends that when they walk they may find treats, they are surprisingly willing and enthusiastic. After your Mini Pig is familiar with walking on a leash, you can put fewer and fewer treats down and eventually none.

Mini Pigs are slow walkers in consequence of their short legs. However, once your pig is trained, they can be a very good walking partner. Just take a gradual approach – start off in the backyard where the area is secure, and your pig is familiar with its' surroundings.

Overtime, you will be ready to take your pig out into your neighborhood, pet store or anywhere you like!

Chapter 13 – Everyday Care

Toilet Training

As with other pets, managing your pig's toileting is part of everyday care. It is relatively easy to train a Micro Pig as pigs tend to go to toilet in the same place all the time.

This means that a pet pig that is kept outside will probably choose their own toileting spot and continue going in this particular place. Even pigs kept indoors will prefer to toilet outside.

To begin training them to toilet outside, simply start taking them out every couple of hours.

Designate an enclosed fenced in area as the toilet area – and take a few steps away to give your pig some space.

As soon as your Mini Pig has been to toilet, take them back inside. This indicates to your piggy that your trip outside was to toilet and not to play.

Make a separate trip outside to play, root and graze but avoid the 'designated toilet area'.

Chapter 13 – Everyday Care

If your Micro Pig lives indoors with you, it is likely that they do not have open access to the outside toilet area. Consider hanging a bell from the door handle of the main door that they use to go out. This way they can alert you to when they need to relieve themselves.

When you take your pig outside in the first few days of training, give the bell a shake. Your Mini Pig will soon associate the sound of the bell with toilet time.

If you feel it is not practical for your Mini Pig to go to toilet outside, you may start with an indoor litter box. This will be especially practical for a very young piglet or when you are experiencing an exceptionally cold winter.

There is currently not a litter box available specifically designed for Mini Pigs. The litter box needs to be sizeable – large enough for your pig to be able to turn around in.

For smaller pigs, a cat litter tray might work well. Some owners have had success using a ferret litter box and have found that the lower front side means that it is easy for piggy to get in and out.

As the pig gets larger, think about using a storage box or even a plastic kiddy pool (you will need to cut an opening in the side so that your pig can step in and out with ease).

Puppy training pads work well to line the litter box. Another alternative is pine shavings or newspaper. Both cedar shavings and cat litter are unsuitable. This is because the cedar shavings are made with oil and the cat litter tends to clump (which may cause a blockage). Unfortunately, your Mini Pig will try eating whatever is lining the litter box. This behavior would be virtually impossible to stop.

Consider where you place the litter box as your pet pig may be very reluctant to adapt to a new position if you try and move it. Perhaps put it somewhere so that it is out of view (behind a piece of furniture).

If your pig has a room of their own, ensure that you put the litter box at the opposite end of the room to their bed. Pigs do not like to sleep near their toileting area.

If you started toilet training inside but feel that your pig is now ready to go outside, simply move the litter box very gradually first towards the door and then just outside it. Keep it a slow process and your pig should be able to adjust gradually.

While toilet training inside, keep your pig in an enclosed area of the house – near and with very easy access to their litter box. Find somewhere that is easy to clean – such as

crate, play pen or small room that you can dedicate to your pet pig.

While cleaning the litter box during toilet training, do not be too overzealous – leave at least one 'pigberry' in the box.

The scent of it will tell your pig that this is the right place to go.

If your Mini Pig is going to toilet where you don't want them to go, try taking one of the 'pigberries' and putting it in the litter box – this should indicate to your pig that you want toileting in the litter box!

Using the litter box usually comes very naturally and instinctively to pigs as they are very clean animals and creatures of habit. This means that you do not need to offer food incentives or rewards. Your pig will find the anticipation of food as a distraction – you want your pig to concentrate on the business of toileting!

A piglet under ten months old will not have full control of their bladder so they will inevitably have accidents. This is when it may be suitable to keep them in a more enclosed area in your house.

If you find that your pig was successfully toilet trained but then starts having accidents again, simply go back to what

you did at the start and keep them in an enclosed area again.

In the first few days of toilet training, walk your Mini Pig to their litter box (whether this is outside or inside) every 2 hours. In the next few days, extend it to 3 hours.

Make sure you are using the same toileting spot every single time. Pigs respond well to routine so make toileting a part of your pig's day – take them to the litter box first thing in the morning, after breakfast, after dinner and before bed.

When your pig does not use the litter box and has a piddle where it shouldn't, simply continue taking them to the litter box every 2 hours. Be patient – being cross with your Mini Pig will not be of any help.

If you are letting your pig go outside to the toilet, make sure they are out for at least 10 minutes.

Avoid giving a snack as a reward for going out to the toilet and then coming in – otherwise they will soon be asking to nip out just so they can come back in to have a treat to eat!

Chapter 13 – Everyday Care

The Importance of Routine

Routine is an important part of your pig's life. A routine enables your pig to know what to expect next. For example, when first waking up in the morning, he / she knows that they will first go toilet, next eat breakfast, next go in the yard etc.

By being able to anticipate what will happen next, your pig is much more likely to be cooperative. They will be happy to go toilet if they know that a meal is coming next.

Try and establish a realistic routine that meets the needs of your pig and is practical for you to be able to commit to. They are probably all things that you would automatically do for your pig but just try to keep the activities in a set order as much as possible.

Activities to include in a routine include meals times, toileting times, one to one training / play / enrichment, nap times, yard play and bed time.

Remember that your routine does not have to be completely rigid but following a certain routine will undoubtedly be of comfort to your Mini Pig.

Your pig will respond well if bedtime is at a similar time each day and, also if you can establish a specific bedtime routine.

Picking Up and Holding

Mini Pigs usually find being picked up a terrifying experience at first. Their prey instinct means that they feel under threat and in danger as soon as your hands reach over them and they feel their feet lift off the ground.

However, once being picked up and held becomes part of their everyday life, they do seem to really enjoy it. You will find cuddling up and holding your Mini Pig strengthens the bond between you both.

In the first few days, it is advisable to avoid lifting your Mini Pig to reduce causing stress and anxiety. It will be a less stressful experience if you can leave picking up your piggy until at least he / she has become familiar with you and learnt to trust you.

However, in some instances, for practical reasons, you may find yourself needing to pick up your pig much sooner than you had intended – if your pig needs help over a step, to reach litter box for example.

Once you have gained the trust of your Mini Pig, and they come when you call, allow them to explore your lap without touching them with your hands.

When your pig seems very comfortable doing this, you can begin to reach (palm upwards) to scratch under the chin or belly. Be patient. If your pig seems nervous or tries to run away, just leave it and try again in a few days.

When your pig feels comfortable with you scratching them underneath their chin and belly, try putting your arms around their body. Once okay with this, you are ready to try and pick them up.

To help your Mini Pig understand what you are doing, say 'up' each time you pick up your pig. Reach (under handed) and lift the pig up and remain in sitting position yourself.

Hold the pig close to you and cradle their body so that you are fully supporting them. Using both your arms, make sure that their legs are tucked in underneath them.

Mini Pigs do love snuggling in blankets so it may help if you wrap your pig in a blanket when you first start picking him / her up.

Your Mini Pig may feel scared and uneasy – they may express this through squealing. Keep hold of your pig, remaining calm and using a very gentle voice.

Persevere – and once your pig begins to calm down, gently put him / her back in your lap. Don't be alarmed, squealing is very normal behavior from your pig. Wait until they feel calm in your arms before freeing them so that they come to learn that you will not do them any harm while holding them.

You want to avoid them thinking that by squealing, you will automatically put them down. Your aim is to get to the point where your Mini Pig enjoys being picked up and held. It will happen – it simply takes time and requires patience.

Treats can be offered to help reassure your Mini Pig that they are not in danger. Wait until your Mini Pig has calmed down while you are holding them and have someone else offer them a treat.

This will involve two people as most important is to keep them secure in both your arms.

Once your Mini Pig feels confident being held on your lap while you are sitting down, you can begin to stand up and later walk holding your pig. Walk very slowly at first.

Your aim will be to remain calm and hold your pig with confidence. This will give your pig some feelings of security.

Once fully grown, it is unlikely that you will be able to hold and carry your Mini Pig. However, it is a very valuable bonding experience when your pig is younger - and one that you are both sure to come to love.

Bathing

Mini Pigs are naturally very clean animals. They have very few sweat glands which means that they do not really have an odor.

If your pig lives primarily in the house and does not tend to get muddy, you will not need to bath them very frequently. However, they will need bathing from time to time - and once bathing is an established part of their routine, many pigs come to relish the experience!

Living in the wild, pigs will often 'do their business' in streams and ponds. Research suggests that this is so that they do not leave a scent that their predators can track down. Unfortunately, this instinctive behavior means that Mini Pigs often toilet as soon as they get their feet wet – as soon as they get in the bathtub or kiddy pool.

To try and eliminate this behavior, try and desensitize your pig to the 'wet feet instinct'. Wipe his / her feet with a wet cloth just before they go toilet (as soon as you enter your designated toileting spot). After they have been toilet, wipe the feet with a wet cloth again.

After a while, your Mini Pig will be so accustomed to wet feet that they will lose their 'wet feet instinct'.

To begin with, take your pig to the bath or shower at least once a day so that they can familiarize themselves with this new environment. Offer a treat but don't worry about any washing to start with.

After a few visits to the bath or shower, you are ready to begin the washing!

There are two ways to try bathing your Mini Pig. Either have the bath run already so that your pig can enjoy a bath. Pigs like the water to be warm but not too hot (a similar temperature to what you would choose for yourself). Otherwise, if you are using a shower cubicle or prefer to, sponge down using a bucket of warm water.

Ensure that your pig is comfortable with being picked up (see previous section) before you try and pick them up to put them in the bathtub.

There will be inevitable squealing for the first few washes. Your Mini Pig is likely to endure stress and feel threatened by the experience. Mini Pigs do not like to feel confined to a certain space or be held in position. This is because, they feel in danger but are not able to run away. You will need to persist through all the squealing.

Once your Mini Pig is in the shower cubicle or bath tub, try and use food as a distraction.

If you run a bath for your pig, you could even float some treats in the water.

Pigs tend to be scared by the running water of the tap so ensure you have done this before leading your pet into the bathroom.

In addition, you do not want the surface of the bath or shower cubicle to feel slippery – place a bathmat or even simply a towel on the bathtub or shower cubicle floor.

If you decide to sponge wash your pig, begin by just washing the feet. Use a bucket filled with warm water. Wash him / her with a cloth or soft sponge. On a subsequent day, begin with feet and work upwards.

Ensure that you do not get water in the ears and be very sensitive around the face.

Plain warm water is absolutely fine but if you prefer, there are shampoos that have been designed for animals. Ultra-mild baby shampoos also work well.

Mini Pigs tend to suffer with very dry skin. Dry them thoroughly and then apply a gentle lotion on them – use baby lotion or oil designed for sensitive skin and / or coconut oil. You could put the oil in a spray bottle and gentle spray a light coat on them.

Bathing can be a very enjoyable experience for your Mini Pig. The more accustomed they become, the more relaxed they will feel.

However, note that baths can contribute to drying out your pig's skin.

Use your judgement on how often to bath your pig. If your pig suffers with very dry skin, you may need to restrict it to one time monthly. Otherwise, you may do it more regularly, especially if your pet pig enjoys it!

Cleaning Ears and Eyes

It is recommended that you routinely clean around the ears and eyes of your Mini Pig.

A brown discharge will collect in the eyelashes and hair around the eyes. Although this is very normal, clean away discharge on a regular basis.

You may even find this brown discharge on their blankets and bed – this is normal for a pig. Use a damp and warm cloth – or if you prefer you could use an eye wash.

Mini Pigs tend to be prone to various eye problems; use this time as a way of thoroughly checking your pig. Contact your Vet with any concerns.

Inside your pig's ears, you will see brown gooey wax. Be extremely careful cleaning around the ears as they are very sensitive.

Chapter 13 – Everyday Care

It is not essential to clean out this wax as he / she will be healthy with or without the wax. The wax actually serves as defense against dust, particles and small insects getting into their ear.

However, if you decide to, only clean the outside edge of the ear. Do not attempt to clean the inner ear area which is enormously sensitive and can be damaged through cleaning.

If you are concerned that your pig has a problem with his / her ears be sure to take them to the Vet.

Use a washcloth or cotton ball moistened with rubbing alcohol or water.

Ensure that the washcloth is only damp – if you squeeze it, there should be no dripping of excess water. It is critical that you do not get water into your pig's ear. This can cause health problems such as head tilt which affects their balance and coordination or an ear infection.

If you have someone to help you, have them provide a treat to keep your pig distracted and calm. This will be easier for you and more pleasant for your Mini Pig. Be prepared for squealing and for your pig to protest to you touching their ears and eyes. Stay calm for the sake of your Mini Pig.

Chapter 13 – Everyday Care

Maintaining Healthy Skin

Naturally, pigs have very dry skin.

Mini Pigs love to be brushed over with a soft bristled brush or grooming glove.

As well as your pig loving the feeling, this also helps to remove the dry flaky skin. Brushing everyday will also help with bonding – at least try to brush 2 – 3 times a week or ideally every day.

If you find that your Mini Pig has particularly dry skin, try limiting the number of baths or washes you give. You can also supplement your Mini Pig feed with a drizzle of flax oil. Put on your pig's food daily and continue brushing until the dry skin begins to improve.

Apply lotion or oil to your pig's skin on a daily basis (not just when your pig has just been bathed). Use a mild baby lotion (non-perfumed) or baby oil and / or coconut oil. Extra virgin olive oil also works really well. Coconut oil can be given with meals, on a teaspoon, with a treat and applied directly to the skin.

Chapter 13 – Everyday Care

When applying any kind of oils, you will need to take extra precautions in the sun after application. Put on extra sunblock straight afterwards.

You may wish to transfer oil into a spray bottle so that you can apply a thin coating of oil all over the skin.

Dehydration may be a cause of your Mini Pig's dry skin condition. Pigs need to drink ample of water, especially in the summertime. If your Miniature Pig seems reluctant to drink, ice provides an interesting incentive. Indeed, a lot of pigs are intrigued by ice – try adding a few cubes to the water bowl to encourage them to drink a little more.

When your pig is out on a sunny day for a considerable length of time, apply sunblock. Your pig will still need plenty of shade available in addition to the sunblock.

Use a children's sunblock with the highest SPF that you can find. Provide access to mud as this also works as a very natural sunblock.

Parasites can also be a cause of extremely dry and flaky skin so ensure that your Mini Pig has been treated for parasites. Obsessive scratching is often an indication of parasites.

Pigs can suffer from skin disorders as a result of a vitamin deficiency. You may need to introduce supplements to their diet to provide whatever is lacking.

Biotin is frequently used to improve skin condition, also fish oil and Vitamin E. It is possible to give too many supplements and vitamins, so it is vital that you consult with your Vet.

Blowing of the Coat

In the Spring or Summertime, Micro Pigs can 'blow their coats'. They do not continually shed fur like a cat or a dog – 'blowing the coat' effectively means shedding a lot of hair over a short time span.

Some lose all their hair while others simply experience some 'hair thinning'. The time period varies amongst Mini Pigs according to genetics, environment and diet.

Regardless of variations, 'blowing the coat' usually happens over a period of weeks or months. The coat blowing allows a seasonal change in their coat.

Once they have shed their hair, they will begin to grow a fresh new coat of hair. You will be able to detect tiny new hairs poking up from their skin.

You will be able to recognize that your Mini Pig is 'blowing their coat' when you see clumps of hair falling off them. Sometimes you will notice significant clumps of hair where they have been sleeping.

This is a normal process and does not indicate any health problems.

Nutritional deficiencies can also cause hair to fall out. Contact your vet if your Mini Pig sheds hair outside of spring and summer time. Also, if they are missing hair around the eyes or if there are just patches of hair missing. This may suggest a medical problem or nutritional deficiency.

Note that Micro Pigs that spend the majority of time indoors (where the temperature is controlled by heating and air conditioning) tend to 'blow the coat' at more random times of the year.

You may notice that your Mini Pig seems to be more agitated during the time of 'blowing the coat'. This can be attributed to itchy and uncomfortable skin due to the hair loss. To ease the discomfort, use a brush to gently remove the loose hair and dead skin.

Most Micro Pigs blow their coats once a year, but it can happen twice a year. Some Micro Pigs will never blow their coats!

Chapter 14 – Food Glorious Food

Diet and Nutrition

Getting the right balance between feeding your pig too much or too little can be very difficult.

Your Mini Pig will adore food to the extent that he / she won't be able to get enough of it. Diet and nutrition is at the absolute heart of keeping your piggy healthy and happy.

Most owners strive to provide a healthy balance of nutritional pellets manufactured for Mini Pigs combined with a variety of vegetables, fruits and other snacks. The manufactured pellets have essential vitamins and minerals in them.

Suggested amounts are usually printed on the bags of feed. The amount depends on the ideal body weight of your Mini Pig.

Note that it does not depend on their actual body weight, but what a pig of their height and weight should be. The recommended serving size should be adjusted to allow for enhancements to the diet such as vegetables, salads, grains, snacks, fruit and grazing.

Mini Pigs up to 25 lbs. – Require ¼ cup pellets 2 x day / Plus a healthy size salad including greens and vegetables / Plus healthy daily snacks.

Mini Pigs over 25 lbs. – Require 2% ideal weight in pellets / Plus a healthy size salad including greens and vegetables / Plus healthy daily snacks.

Chapter 14 – Food Glorious Food

Just like people, every pig is different and will have different dietary requirements. A pig that is more active will need more food intake than one that spends most of the time resting.

An essential part of your pig's diet is the fresh vegetables that need to be provided in addition to the formulated food. A decent variety of fresh vegetables should make up about 25% of your pig's diet.

Good choices of vegetables include cucumber, carrot, celery, peppers and greens. Although fruits are healthy, they have a high sugar content so can only be given in moderation.

The majority of Mini Pigs adore apples, grapes and raisins. These could be reserved as treats for good behavior and in training.

An alternative to using formulated feed is a completely natural diet. To ensure that all the vital vitamins and minerals are provided, you will need to include a wide variety of foods from different sources.

Protein high foods include; almonds, peanuts, beechnuts, brazil nuts, butternuts, cashew nut, flaxseed, hazel nuts, sunflower seeds, pumpkin seeds, pecan nuts, and walnuts; cereal grains such as oats, quinoa, brown rice, oat bran, wheat bran, barley, corn and hominy; beans (cooked and not raw) like kidney beans, lima beans, pinto beans.

Note that pigs really enjoy parts of the vegetables and fruits that we are accustomed to discarding in the garbage. Feed them peelings, the cores of cabbage, lettuce and apples, banana peelings. Pigs are not able to consume the peel from citrus fruits although they do enjoy citrus fruits that have been peeled.

Unsuitable items to feed your Mini Pig include cat or dog food, meat, alcoholic drinks, chocolate, salty foods, candies or sugary treats, acorns, dairy products or poisonous plants. Ensure that what you give your pig has nutritional value – they will not thrive on foods that are simply empty calories.

Assess the size and shape of your Mini Pig to check that you are not over or under feeding.

You should not be able to see the spine or hip bones of your Mini Pig – they should have a well-rounded backside.

If you notice that your piggy is gaining weight quickly, it is likely that you need to cut back on the quantity that you are feeding.

Likewise, if you see that your piggy is not gaining weight, it is likely that you will need to increase the quantity you are feeding.

Feeding less than the recommended manufacturers guidelines or restricting feed in an effort to reduce growth will cause severe suffering to your Mini Pig. It will cause permanent damage to organs and will inevitably result in a shorter lifespan.

Mini Pigs require calories and nutrients to maintain good health and to be active and inquisitive.

Measure all your pig's food so that you know what is being consumed.

It may be beneficial to take your pre-measured amount of food and allow your pig to graze on it throughout the day as opposed to having 2 – 3 larger meals.

Where possible, try and allow your pig to forage for their food. Provide multiple smaller meals instead of 'main meals'.

Remember that you will need something to put in your rooting box – or sand box; plus, food for rewards and incentives for training and more food for a variety of enrichment activities!

All needs to be measured to ensure you are providing the necessary quantity.

This will be a closer imitation of how a wild pig would feed. They would spend the day roaming around and rooting for food. They would need to work for it – and not have it from a big bowl placed in front of them.

Providing food that can be foraged is likely to be a healthier and happier way for your Mini Pig to feed.

Feeding will become a fulfilling activity rather than simply a meal from the dish.

Chapter 14 – Food Glorious Food

Healthy Foodstuffs

The following is a comprehensive list of foods that are healthy for your Micro Pig;

Vegetables

Acorn Squash

Artichoke

Arugula

Asparagus

Banana Squash

Bamboo Shoots

Beets

Bok Choy

Broccoli

Brussel Sprouts

Burdock Root

Buttercup Squash

Butternut Squash

Cabbage

Carrots

Celery

Chayote Squash

Chickweed

Chives

Collard Greens

Corn (Restrict intake as the pellets include high proportion of corn)

Cucumber

Dandelion (flowers and leaves)

Eggplant

Endive

Fennel

Galangal Root

Green Bean

Green Soybean (Edamame)

Jicama

Kale

Kohlrabi

Leek

Lettuce

Mustard Greens

Okra

Olives (Limit consumption due to sodium content)

Parsnip

Peas (including pods)

Peanut

Pepper

Pumpkin

Radicchio

Radish (and leaves)

Rutabagas

Salsify

Shallots

Sorrel

Spinach

Squash

Sweet Potatoes

Swiss Chard

Tomatoes (Note that the plant and leaves are poisonous)

Turnip (Including the green leaves)

Wasabi Root

Watercress

Winged Beans

Yucca Root

Zucchini

Fruit

Apples (remove seeds)

Apricots (remove pits)

Banana (including peel)

Bitter Melon

Black Currants

Blackberries

Blueberries

Boysenberries

Breadfruit

Cactus Pear

Cantaloupe Melon

Cape Gooseberries

Cherimoya

Cherries (remove pits)

Clementines (remove peel)

Coconut

Crab Apples

Cranberries (fresh or dried)

Dates

Durian

Elderberries (blue and purple feijoa)

Figs

Grapefruit

Grapes (to avoid choking hazard, cut in half lengthways)

Guava

Honeydew Melon

Huckleberries

Jackfruit

Jujube (also known as red date)

Kiwi (including peel)

Kumquats

Lemon

Lime

Loganberries

Lychee

Mango

Mulberries

Nectarine (remove pit)

Olallieberries

Orange (remove peel)

Papaya

Passion Fruit

Peaches (remove pit)

Pears (remove seeds)

Chapter 14 – Food Glorious Food

Persimmons

Pineapple

Plums (remove pit)

Pomegranate

Pumelo

Quince

Raspberries

Red Banana

Redcurrants

Sapodillas

Sharon Fruit

Star Fruit

Strawberries

Tangerines (remove peel)

Thimbleberries

Watermelon (including rind)

Grains

Amaranth

Barley

Buckwheat

Brown Rice (cooked)

Corn

Faro

Freekeh

Millet

Oats / Oatmeal

Quinoa

Rye

Sorghum

Teff

Wheat Varieties

Spelt

Emmer

Faro

Einkorn

Durum

Bulgar

Cracked Wheat

Wheat Berries

Nuts and Seeds (Unsalted)

Almonds

Cashews

Chia Seeds

Cumin Seeds

Black Oil Sunflower Seeds

Brazil Nuts

Flax Seeds (not too many)

Grape Seeds

Hazelnuts

Hemp Seeds

Macadamia Nuts

Papaya Seeds

Peanuts

Pecans

Pistachios

Pomegranate Seeds

Pumpkin Seeds

Sesame Seeds

Sunflower Seeds

Walnuts (deshelled)

Wheat Germ

Legumes (MUST be cooked and NO canned beans)

Alfalfa

Black Beans

Black Eyed Peas

Boston Beans

Chick Peas

Fava Beans (also known as broad beans)

Field Peas

Kidney Beans

Lentils

Lima Beans

Mayocoba Beans

Mung Beans

Navy Beans

Pinto Beans

Red Beans

Split Peas

Suitable Special Treats

Applesauce (without sugar)

Baby food (sugar and salt free)

Fruit Chips (banana, apple)

Coconut Oil

Coconut Water

Cottage Cheese

Eggs (scrambled or hard boiled)

Fruit Juice (with no added sugar)

Granola

Oatmeal (cooked)

Peanut Butter on celery

Popcorn (air popped, no oils, butter or seasoning)

Pumpkin (whole or canned pumpkin with nothing extra added)

Yogurt (plain)

Poisonous Foodstuffs

Acorns and oak leaves

Almond – wild almonds are toxic but the almonds available in stores have been heat treated to eliminate toxicity.

Apple (leave and seeds)

Apricot (leaves and pit)

Avocado (skin and pit)

Broccoli (roots and seeds)

Cabbage (roots and seeds)

Cashews (raw) – cashew nuts available in stores are not raw.

Cassava (roots and leaves)

Castor Beans

Cherry (leaves and pit)

Corn Stalks

Elderberries (red berries)

Kidney Beans (raw or improperly cooked)

Lima Beans (raw or improperly cooked)

Longan (seeds)

Lychee (seeds)

Mustard (roots and seeds)

Nectarine (leaves and pit)

Nutmeg (large quantities)

Peach (leaves and pit)

Pear (leaves and seeds)

Plum (leaves and pit)

Potato (green parts of potato and leaves)

Salt

Sweet Potatoes (decayed / black parts)

Taro (raw)

Tobacco (leaves)

Tomato (leaves and vine)

Rambutan (raw seeds)

Rhubarb (leaves)

Walnut Shells (moldy)

Hydration

It is of critical importance for a Micro Pig to drink enough fluids.

Lack of hydration tends to be the main cause of dry and irritable skin and is essential for good health. Some owners find that their Mini Pigs do not drink enough water, especially in the hotter months.

Dehydration can cause health problems including kidney troubles, urinary tract infections as well as constipation.

Many pigs enjoy ice, so this may be a way to encourage your Mini Pig to drink more water.

Also consider putting treats that float on water in the water bowl (such as cheerios, diced carrots). The same can be done in the kiddie pool – they will be drinking as they look for and consume the floating (or sunk!) snacks.

If you are concerned about low water intake, increase provision of vegetables that have a high-water content. Good examples include cucumber, celery, lettuce (not iceberg), zucchini or yellow squash. Watermelon is great but needs to be given in moderation because of the high sugar content.

Another trick is to soak their pellets in water. As well as providing additional water and increased hydration, the water soaked pellets will make your Mini Pig feel fuller quicker.

Ensure that the water you are providing for your Micro Pig is lovely and clean. Pigs will refuse water that is dirty or smells. Biofilm can build up in a dirty water dish and this will cause health problems.

Some Mini Pigs are insistent on tipping over their water bowls! Consider investing in a tip proof bowl – look for one that is seriously heavy.

Some owners even add concrete to the underside of the water bowl so that it is much more difficult to tip over. Out in the yard, consider sinking a container of water into the ground.

Also scatter several bowls around the yard and in the home – being easily available will encourage your Mini Pig to drink more.

Pigs find it difficult to regulate salt / sodium in their bodies so they are vulnerable to salt poisoning.

The risk will be minimized where they are provided with a constant supply of clean drinking water. Mini Pigs can suffer from salt poisoning through their diet (salty snacks) and salt poisoning through dehydration / water deprivation.

Dehydration is the most common form of salt poisoning. Fresh clean water needs to be provided always.

Chapter 15 – Piggy Healthcare

Photosensitivity and Sunburn

Micro Pigs are very susceptible to sunburn, and affected skin will be painful, also leaving them prone to secondary infections.

Always use sunblock as the rays of the sun are harmful for Mini Pigs just as they are to humans. Like humans, Mini Pigs can develop skin cancer.

Find a sunblock with a high SPF that is mild and suitable for sensitive skin. Children's sunscreens usually work well. Apply frequently – as much as every 30 minutes when exposed to the sun.

Provide plenty of shade as discussed in our section 'Providing Protection' (Chapter 8 – Becoming Piggy Prepared).

Additionally, the importance of mud should not be underestimated. Mud provides necessary protection from the sun (refer to section 'Glorious Mud' in Chapter 10 - Enriching the Life of your Mini Pig). Mud works as a fabulous natural sunscreen.

UV radiation is not the only cause of sunburn. Consumption of certain plants will cause a Micro Pig to develop photosensitivity – effectively the Micro Pig's skin becomes increasingly sensitive to the ultra violet radiation from the sun. This affects all Micro Pigs that spend any length of time outdoors.

This photosensitivity is caused by a reaction to chlorophyll. Chlorophyll is present in some wheat plants – this generates a toxin that increases sensitivity to the sun.

This results in much more severe sunburn and will even cause a Mini Pig to burn in the shade.

The disease causes a reddening (or erythema) over the white areas that are exposed to the rays of the sun. The affected areas of skin are damaged and become coagulated with serum – this is followed by a secondary bacterial infection where a thick crust forms.

This is very painful for the Mini Pig and they will need to be moved indoors away from any sunlight. The pig will need to see their vet for antibiotic treatment.

It is of crucial importance that you check your yard to see if you have any plants that may cause photosensitivity.

Chapter 15 – Piggy Healthcare

Plants to avoid include;

Bishop's Weed

Parsnip tops

Parsley

Celery tops

Giant Hog Weed

Buckwheat

Saint John's Wort

Hoof Care

Hoof trimming is a vital part of a Mini Pig's health. The length of the hooves effects the way a pig walks and any delay in getting hooves trimmed can cause long lasting health problems.

Some pigs will only need their hooves trimmed once a year while others will need trimming more regularly.

Try handling and filing their hooves from a young age. Even though a young piglet will not need hoof trimming, begin the process of desensitization. This will allow them to trust you in touching their hooves ready for hoof trimming. This is highly valuable as the Mini Pig grows older and larger.

Check hooves and pads daily. Look for cracks, splits and any overgrowth. Once this established as a routine, you will be able to use a nail file to gently scratch the surface of your pig's hoof. Use cuticle cutters to trim the very tip of the hoof.

In this way, you are gradually working up to hoof trims where you use hoof trimmers.

If you are experienced and confident, this is something that you can do yourself. With a piglet, you can use a hard wire cutter, large nail cutter and high grit emery board. When the pig grows old, hooves will become thicker and tougher. Consequently, tools need to be stronger and you would use hoof clippers, trimmers, hoof file.

However, most owners tend to take their Micro Pig to the vet for regular hoof trimming.

To minimize the need for hoof trimming, provide opportunities for your piggy to walk on rough surfaces. This will help to wear the hooves down naturally. Pavement / cement will help as well as lots of walking and physical activity.

Dental Care

Another critical aspect to your Mini Pig's health is dental care. Make regular checks of their mouth, teeth and gums. Establish this dental check as part of their routine. It will be easier if you are able to do this from a very young age.

Some owners like to brush their Micro Pig's teeth. This can help to avoid gum and dental diseases. You can use either a toothbrush or a washcloth – whichever you choose, start from as young as you can.

Start by simply putting the toothbrush with or without toothpaste in their mouth and leave it in there for about 5 seconds. Gradually increase the amount of time and begin to actually brush the teeth.

You need to be able to trust your Mini Pig to do this – they can bite. It is not necessary and may be impractical if the Mini Pig did not become accustomed to teeth brushing as a piglet.

You can simply use a toothbrush or washcloth, but you can also use a cleanser. Both baking soda and fluoride free toothpaste would both work well. Just ensure that any toothpaste is free from fluoride as this is toxic for pigs (and humans).

Chew toys are a fantastic way to improve your Mini Pig's dental health. Ensure that the toys you provide are safe for pigs and toxin free.

If your pet pig seems uninterested in a chew toy, try to make it more appetizing by filling them with treats. Many manufacturers make edible chew toys that are designed to enhance dental health. The action of gnawing on the chew toy can eradicate some soft tartar and is good stimulation for their gums.

If you feel unable to clean your Mini Pig's teeth, your vet will be able to for you. They will also be able to provide you with guidance and usually, a demonstration.

Just like baby humans, piglets begin to teeth at around 1 year old. They can experience discomfort during this time so can be irritable – and / or grind their teeth. Some owners provide their pig with teething items that are available from pet stores.

Another idea is to make some ice cubes; use a mixture of water, juice, yogurt, bits of fruit and veg. This can be very soothing. Your piglet will lose their baby teeth so that their adult teeth can grow through. You may find the teeth that have fallen out – they look like broken pieces of tooth, but they are the baby teeth.

Piglets are born with 8 very sharp 'needle' teeth. These will normally be clipped by the breeder or veterinarian before the piglet comes home with you. These baby teeth are incredibly sharp and so can easily hurt people (or other piglets or pigs).

If you are concerned that these teeth have not already been clipped, speak to your vet.

These 'needle' teeth will fall out and be replaced by permanent teeth at approximately 8 – 12 months old. Clipping or removing these teeth has no impact on tusk growth.

The complete set is made up of 44 teeth. Pigs under a year old have 28 teeth – they will lose 14 of these.

Tusk Care

Both male and female pigs grow tusks, including those that have been neutered or spayed. Tusk growth is driven by testosterone. This means that an unaltered boar will have the fastest growth of tusk, next a neutered male and unaltered female, and slowest of all, the spayed female.

There is no exact age when tusks begin to develop, but it usually happens at around 2 – 3 years of age. Female tusks cease to grow at maturity and the tusk root closes. Neutered males will have tusks that protrude from the mouth. The tusk of the males continually grows throughout an entire lifespan.

It is generally considered that instead of removing the tusks, it is more advisable that your vet files and trims them regularly. However, males are inclined to tusk root abscesses because of trimming them and exposing the pulp – if tusks are growing in such a way that they are not posing a threat to the pig or to you as the owner, it may be advisable not to trim them at all.

How often a Mini Pig needs their tusk trimming varies between individual pigs. Tusks grow at different rates, perhaps in response to testosterone levels. The majority of Micro Pig's need tusk trimming from between 1 and 3 years old. Some will require yearly trims, and some will need it more frequently.

Some owners choose to leave the tusks alone, but you do need to consider safety. Mini Pigs living alongside children and other animals may cause an injury, intentionally or unintentionally.

The tusks are seriously sharp – they could create a lot of damage even if somebody came a little too close to the tusk.

And, your Mini Pig will be much more dangerous if he / she does display any aggressive behaviors.

Also, if the tusk grows in such a way that it is uncomfortable or painful for your Mini Pig, you will obviously need the tusk trimming and will not have a choice.

Tusk trimming needs to be undertaken by someone with experience and so most owners take their Micro Pig to the veterinarian for regular tusk trimming.

The tusk should never be removed completely as they form part of the jawbone – any removal would have serious health consequences. Your vet will sedate / anesthetize your pet pig during the procedure. It is important that the tusk is not trimmed too closely to the gum line – at least ½ inch or more of tusk should be left.

Health Benefits of Sterilizing

There are important health benefits to having your Micro Pig spayed or neutered. Not spaying or neutering is the prime cause of behavioral problems that then leads to the pig being abandoned and without a home and family.

Leaving the pig unaltered carries a far greater risk than the procedure itself. It is advisable to spay or neuter your Mini Pig while they are young. The procedure for older pigs is more expensive and has added complications.

Please note that most veterinarians advise that pigs should not be given any food after midnight on the day before surgery. Consult with your vet and follow their recommendation.

Females – It is recommended that female pigs are spayed between 4 – 6 months of age.

When females are not sterilized, they can become sexually irritated and aggressive in line with heat cycles every 21 days. While in heat, they will mark their territory by urinating – wherever they happen to be including all over the home (this is true of the most reliably potty-trained piggy).

While in heat, females also tend to behave aggressively and will fight with other pig pets or any other pet animals. They will try to mount and hump anyone they choose, including children. This can be dangerous as your piggy becomes heavier.

This behavior cannot be changed through training – the pigs will be driven completely by their hormones. Despite training, they will bite, lunge, charge and jump and the pig will not be able to control their behavior.

Unaltered female pigs are also more likely to develop reproductive cancers, such as ovarian, mammary and uterine. Other risks to health include infections such as pyometra and mastitis. These are serious health risks.

Males – It is recommended that males are neutered between 8 – 12 weeks old. Without sterilizing, male pigs (boars) make for very unsuitable pets. Boars are controlled by their hormones; they will hump, ejaculate (on you, furniture, carpet, other pets, guests, toys etc.), they will behave aggressively and are much more likely to try and escape (as they are desperate to seek a mate). This is all a result of their sexual frustration.

Their tusks would grow incredibly fast and dangerously long - and so would need extremely frequent trimming.

Unaltered males release a terrible odor when they are excited or scared. Urine would have a very strong smell due to the prepuce gland and they would likely be inclined to urinate around their home environment in the hope of leaving a scent for a female pig.

Unaltered boars also have an overpowering musky odor that is very unpleasant to humans.

There is an increased risk of health issues with males that have not been neutered. He is more inclined to develop testicular cancer, suffer with prostate infections and preputial ulcers.

After Surgery - Subsequent to surgery, your beloved Micro Pig will need plenty of peace and quiet. Keep your piggy warm after surgery, as he / she will find it difficult to regulate their temperature.

It is likely that your pig will feel nauseous due to the anesthesia so only offer small portions of food for the rest of the day. Hydration will be important so, as usual, have plenty of fresh clean water available. Water will prevent constipation and assist the whole body in functioning properly.

The only time a pig will be reluctant to eat is if they are in pain. It is important to control your pig's pain as there is a risk of an ulcer developing when they feel stressed and they go without food for a considerable length of time.

Follow your veterinarian's advice on pain management and offer lots of small meals throughout the day. Provide foodstuffs that are easy to digest – canned pumpkin, applesauce, yogurt, cottage cheese, peanut butter, water rich fruits and vegetables such as watermelon and cucumber.

Ensure that you give food with all medicines that you give to your Micro Pig. This will help to protect their stomach.

The following day, your pig will likely be ready to return to meals and snacks as usual. But avoid opportunities for your Mini Pig to run, jump and climb for at least 2 days.

It is usually recommended that pigs stay away from water – baths and pools for approximately 10 days. This will help recovery and healing.

After a spay, a female will sometimes have some accidents. This is quite normal since her ovaries are located right below her bladder. This will automatically stop as she heals, and her controlling muscles become strong again.

Be sure to ask your veterinarian for any advice or tips. Check on the incision daily and consult your vet with any concerns, however minor they may be.

It will be a few weeks before the hormones dissipate. Behaviors and odors will remain unchanged for another couple of weeks. Males will still be fertile for about 2 weeks after surgery and females will continue to mark their territory by urinating.

Patience is the only solution – behaviors will gradually begin to improve as the hormones become much less dominating and compelling for your pig.

Common Health Problems

Annual vaccinations and regular check-ups will help to avoid many health problems. Look out for any unusual changes in your Micro Pig's physical appearance, behavior and eating habits – respond quickly by seeking advice from your veterinarian. It is better to deal with a problem at the start rather than waiting until it has become a major health problem.

Obesity – Pigs adore food with a passion and are driven by their absolute obsession with it. They will stop at nothing to try and have an extra treat from any source. Consequently, you need to carefully monitor your feeding plan to ensure that you are not overfeeding your Mini Pig.

Obesity is such a critical issue as it leads to many other health problems.

It contributes to chronic lameness and blindness (resulting from excessive fat which accumulates around the eyes). Obesity also puts great strain on the heart and lungs. Additionally, obese pigs are more vulnerable to heat stress when out in the sun or inside a warm and cozy home.

Lack of exercise is also a fundamental cause of obesity. By scattering food or hiding in a toy or rooting box, you will be encouraging your pet pig to use up extra calories – and will experience both physical and mental stimulation.

Equally important though, is not to underfeed your Micro Pig as this will also cause suffering and permanent health problems.

Ensure that your pig is provided with the correct quantity of calories and adequate nutrition. Refer to '**Chapter 14 Food Glorious Food'** and look at the section on **'Diet and Nutrition'**.

For further support, ask your vet for recommendations. They may be able to provide you with a suggested feeding plan.

Respiratory Illness – Miniature pigs tend to suffer with respiratory and nasal infections.

One of the most frequent health problems is atrophic rhinitis; this is a nasal passage infection. Watch out for a nasal discharge or constant runny nose. In severe cases, blood can be discharged from the nose. The pig will be at risk of permanent nasal deformities.

To prevent this, ensure that you keep up with regular vaccinations. The vaccinations eliminate the organisms which cause this problem. Also, be vigilant where a pig begins to experience nasal discharge. Always seek medical attention from a vet.

Pneumonia is another problem for miniature pigs. Symptoms to look out for include coughing, lethargy, and fever. This is a very serious problem and you will need to medical help from your vet immediately.

Arthritis and Osteoarthritis – As a Miniature Pig ages, arthritis and osteoarthritis (joint degeneration) becomes quite common. It is often the result of chronic obesity and / or overgrown hooves.

If your pig appears to be lame, consult with your vet as medication can be prescribed to help with the pain and inflammation. However continuing lameness will become unresponsive to anti-inflammatories and pain killers over time. This is a common reason for euthanasia in the older pig.

By ensuring that your Micro Pig is of good weight and not obese, you will be decreasing the chances of arthritis.

Skin Problems – This tends to be an ongoing problem which affects all Miniature Pigs. They are very susceptible to sunburn and virtually all pigs will experience some level of dry and itchy skin. To help ease dry skin, use mild moisturizing lotions.

Melanoma (skin cancer) can affect pigs. Be watchful for any type of growth and consult with vet if you have any concerns.

Urinary Tract Problems – Micro Pigs are susceptible to cystitis, bladder infections and stones in the bladder. If you notice that your pig seems to be in pain and straining to urinate, contact your vet quickly.

Antibiotics can be prescribed for cystitis and emergency surgery may be required if there are stones in the bladder causing the urethra to be blocked.

Constipation – This is a frequent problem for pigs. Be alert for signs of straining to defecate and be observant of their excretory output.

Dehydration is a common cause of constipation. Make water readily and conveniently available. If you are concerned that your pig is still not drinking enough, provide water rich foods. Plus, you could add a little juice to their water. Just be aware that once you have added juice to their water, they may be even more reluctant to have plain water in the future.

Constipation can also result from consumption of a foreign object which may require removal by the vet.

Extended straining, resulting from constipation, can cause a rectal prolapse which will require surgical intervention.

Dental Disease – Older male pigs are prone to tusk root abscessation. This is likely to first appear as a chin or jaw abscess – but that recurs after the initial treatment. The tusk will need to be removed through surgery including removal of part of the jaw that the tusk is embedded into.

Pigs tend to accumulate a high level of dental tartar as they become older. Severe periodontal disease is not common, but some pigs may benefit from regular teeth cleaning (see section **'Dental Care'** earlier in this Chapter).

Uterine Neoplasia – This affects female pigs that have not been sterilized. Indeed, most unaltered females will develop these neoplasms. Some are benign, but some will be cancerous. These masses can grow to the extent that pressure is put on the heart and lungs. This pressure alone can cause significant health problems.

Consequently, the mass will need to be removed, cancerous or not.

You will be able to prevent this health problem by having your female pig spayed.

Afterword

The world of Mini Pigs is without doubt, a complex one.

On the one hand pigs are a remarkably loving pet, capable of following rules and learning new tricks. On the other hand, their obsession with food drives them to do anything for it – be it positive or negative behavior.

Their intelligence and high sociability both makes them a wonderful companion but one who will be heavily emotionally dependent on you and your family.

Unquestionably, a highly rewarding companion but one who will make incredible demands on you which is not always easy in our busy lives.

These Micro Pigs are realistically not mini at all – simply significantly smaller than the average farm pigs. When you are cooing over a Micro Piglet, just remember how big they grow.

You will need space to accommodate them in your home – your pet pig plus all the necessary accessories – beds, crate, playpens and more. Practical adaptations may need to be made such as a ramp built where there are steps.

Afterword

Additionally, part of your yard will need to be devoted to mud with a safe and secure area purely for your pig.

Add to the natural demands of the Micro Pig, you also must consider Zoning Laws and other rules regarding keeping livestock in your accommodation (or future home). There are legal obligations too when travelling with your pig.

Consider carefully whether you can make such a commitment. After all, this is a responsibility which may last for 10 to 15 years. A fascinating and rewarding pet without question but one which requires much more dedication than the average pet.

Training is an absolute requirement and needs to be continued throughout their life. This makes an incredibly interesting pet but only for the most dedicated owners.

Think about your household. Mini Pigs are very sociable creatures and will enjoy another piggy companion. This will inevitably require more space being given to the pigs and more of your time.

Alternatively, the Mini Pig may be able to socialize with other pets in your household but consider carefully whether you think this is likely to work. Although Mini Pigs can get along well with dogs, bad relationships (particularly

Afterword

between dogs and Mini Pigs) is very often the reason that pigs end up in sanctuaries and in need of a new home.

It is not always easy to incorporate a Miniature Pig into a home with young children. The pig will need reminding that it is not in charge of your child (or children). As the adult owner, you will need to supervise play between child and pig and help to reinforce the hierarchy of your household; teaching your pig its' place in the herd.

Hopefully this book has guided you through the pros and cons of owning a pet pig. It should help you in making this difficult decision. After all, you want to be sure for the sake of the pig. Now that you are knowledgeable, you are in a superb position to make a realistic decision. Help spread the word and hopefully, with a better educated public, there will be a dramatic decline in the number of Miniature Pigs ending up in a Shelter.

Whether you decide to become a 'Piggy Parent' or you are simply a 'Piggy Admirer', we can all still enjoy finding out as much as we can about this fascinating and heartwarming animal. The very fact that it is so demanding makes it so incredibly captivating.

Index

Index

Index

Made in the USA
Coppell, TX
14 December 2020